T0378368

Combating Antisemitism

in Germany and Poland

Combating Antisemitism in Germany and Poland

Strategies Since 1990

Thomas Just

LYNNE
RIENNER
PUBLISHERS

BOULDER
LONDON

Published in the United States of America in 2024 by
Lynne Rienner Publishers, Inc.
1800 30th Street, Suite 314, Boulder, Colorado 80301
www.rienner.com

and in the United Kingdom by
Lynne Rienner Publishers, Inc.
1 Bedford Row, London WC1R 4BU
www.eurospanbookstore.com/rienner

Library of Congress Cataloging-in-Publication Data
A Cataloging-in-Publication record for this book
is available from the Library of Congress.

ISBN 978-1-68585-999-2 (hc)

British Cataloguing in Publication Data
A Cataloguing in Publication record for this book
is available from the British Library.

Printed and bound in the United States of America

The paper used in this publication meets the requirements
∞ of the American National Standard for Permanence of
Paper for Printed Library Materials Z39.48-1992.

5 4 3 2 1

Contents

Tables and Figures

Tables

Figures

Acknowledgments

IN THE SUMMER OF 2010, I BECAME ONE OF THE FEW AMERICAN STU-
dents to serve as an intern within Poland's Ministry of Foreign Affairs.
While I did not know it at the time, this experience would change the
trajectory of my career. Among the issues I was tasked with researching
were ways that the Polish government could better conduct outreach to
Jewish communities inside Poland and abroad. What I found was that,
while Poland had been working to reconcile with the tragedy of the
Holocaust, the legacy of antisemitism remained a major obstacle that
continued to reopen wounds some seventy years later. I would like to
thank my supervisors, in particular Maciej Kozłowski and Sebastian
Rejak, for opening my eyes to and sparking my interest in this crucially
important topic.

During my time in Poland, I would occasionally reflect on my
past experiences in Germany and how issues of antisemitism and the
Holocaust were treated across the border. I often was struck by how
the events of World War II and the Holocaust continue to impact the
national consciousness of both countries. I had previously spent an
academic year studying at Leipzig University and a summer at the
Dresden University of Technology, as well as a summer at the
Leopoldinum Gymnasium in Passau. My memories of these experiences inspired me to further investigate what efforts Germany had
made to reconcile with its own history and the legacy of antisemitism
within the country. In doing so, I learned that while both of these
countries had developed strategies to combat antisemitism, there had
not yet been a comprehensive study conducted to evaluate whether or

not these approaches actually made progress. This realization led me to undertake this project.

Research in the area of antisemitism is interdisciplinary, requiring a knowledge of history, politics, religion, language, and data literacy. I would like to thank several individuals who equipped me with the tools necessary to carry out this project. I especially thank two professors from my time at Baylor University, Andrew Wisely and Jennifer Good, as well as the most impactful teacher during my time as a K–12 student, Mark Wagner of Nicolet High School. My ability to read and contextualize the data used in the book is in large part thanks to studying under Angela Hawken at Pepperdine University. I would also like to thank Tatiana Kostadinova at Florida International University, whose feedback and guidance were instrumental in the early stages of this project, as well as John Clark, Tudor Parfitt, and Markus Thiel, also at Florida International University.

A significant portion of my research was conducted during my time as a fellow at the Martin-Springer Institute at Northern Arizona University. I would like to thank the institute's director, Björn Krondorfer, for his mentorship, and the generosity of Jeanette Garretty Reinhard for creating the fellowship. In the final stages of production, the book benefited greatly from the advice and recommendations of the editorial staff at Lynne Rienner Publishers. Additionally, I am grateful to my colleagues at Arizona State University and the Future Security Initiative for offering their support, supplying insights, and providing me with opportunities to connect with scholars from around the world and present my work in various forums.

Not least, I thank my family and friends. I am fortunate to have an incredible support system behind me and people who allow me to have a life outside and beyond my work. I am especially grateful to my parents, Thomas Just Sr. and Susan Stone, and grandparents, Esther Just, James Patrick and Dianne Robertson, and Barbara and T. J. Holtgrieve. Without their love and support, none of this would have been possible.

1

Combating Antisemitism in Germany and Poland

ANTISEMITISM IS A HATRED THAT DATES BACK MILLENNIA AND HAS BEEN responsible for millions of murders. Antisemitism has left especially deep scars on the history and identity of central Europe—the location of one of the largest, most systematic genocides in history. Memories of the Holocaust continue to influence the social and political affairs of Germany and Poland. This is particularly true as extremist groups from a variety of ideological perspectives continue to revive and perpetuate antisemitic myths and conspiracy theories and to carry out acts of violence. As a response, the governments of these countries have recently taken steps to address the problem, such as making Holocaust denial illegal, granting Judaism legal status on par with Christianity, and facilitating the revival of domestic Jewish organizations. However, no comprehensive study has yet assessed the effectiveness of these efforts. The primary goal of this book is to evaluate these two countries' approaches and provide some new paths forward.

The importance of work in this area has only increased with the resurgence of nationalist ideologies, conspiracy theories, and prejudices reminiscent of those prior to World War II. While conflicts throughout history have resulted in the rise and fall of various political and social movements, the ideologies behind such movements tend to never fully disappear. Fascism and Nazism may have been defeated on the battlefield in the 1940s, but central elements to such ideologies continue to linger within extremist movements that may or may not go by a different name. Even as memorials to the Holocaust are now a common sight throughout many central European cities and the mantra of "never

1

again" is repeated frequently, the same manifestations of antisemitism that have existed for centuries persist.

Two central questions are explored in this book. First, what are the primary ways in which antisemitism tends to manifest? Second, what strategies have been employed in these two countries to counter antisemitic hatred, and have they been effective? Germany and Poland are especially ripe for such research given their historical memories of the Holocaust and efforts to reconcile with the past. The Holocaust has in many ways contributed to defining each country's modern identity. Because of this, both countries have had immense motivation to address antisemitism—not only to reduce crime and violence domestically, but also to improve international perceptions about their respective histories and national identities.

Defining Antisemitism

Before we can begin answering the questions posed here, it is important to establish a common understanding of what antisemitism is. The *Merriam-Webster Dictionary* (2023) defines *antisemitism* as "hostility toward or discrimination against Jews as a religious, ethnic, or racial group." Such a definition conveys the broad nature of the term; however, a better understanding of its meaning requires examination of the ways in which antisemitism tends to manifest itself. Various manifestations of antisemitism throughout history have each carried distinct, yet often related forms of discrimination, stereotypes, and hatred. The term becomes even more complex when considering the ways in which these manifestations have evolved over time. In this section, I will conceptualize what antisemitism is and provide a more accurate definition to be used throughout this analysis.

While numerous organizations have developed their own definitions of antisemitism, these tend to differ greatly in terms of describing how antisemitism manifests itself.[1] As part of this study, I have developed a concise operational definition that emphasizes four categories that I believe best encapsulate the primary manifestations of antisemitism. These categories can most succinctly be described as religious, economic, racial, and political. Each of these categories has developed on a different timeline from one another, but an understanding of each is necessary to fully grasp the nature of contemporary antisemitism. In order to develop a more precise definition of antisemitism, this section will explain each of these manifestations and its development.

Religious Antisemitism

Many historians regard religious antisemitism as the oldest manifestation dating back to antiquity. The origins of antisemitism are often traced to Jews' refusal to adopt majority religious and social practices in ancient Egypt. Numerous Egyptian and Greek historians of this era depicted the religious practices of Jews as absurd and inhospitable. Religious antisemitism evolved centuries later as early Christians placed heavy blame on Jews for the crucifixion of Jesus—an accusation of deicide. Some of this was fueled by New Testament writings, such as "the Jews who killed the Lord Jesus and the prophets and also drove us out. They displease God and are hostile to everyone" (1 Thessalonians 2:14–15 [NIV]). Scholars differ as to the precise meaning and background of such passages, but these passages have nonetheless played a role in Christian-Jewish tensions throughout history. Because of this, Jews were often portrayed as representing the devil in medieval European paintings, restricted to socially inferior occupations, and subjected to blood libels (Cohen, 2007: 208). Certain Christian thinkers, such as Martin Luther, perpetuated antisemitic beliefs by describing Jews as "base, whoring people, that is, no people of God" and "full of devil's feces" (Luther, trans. 1971: 20; Michael, 2006: 113). Such religiously based manifestations of antisemitism have been a point of tension between Christians and Jews, particularly in Europe, for millennia.

It is, however, a bit more difficult to pinpoint the religious origins of Islamic antisemitism. Unlike in Christian texts, the Quran does not accuse Jews of deicide. Thus, the religious nature of antisemitism in Islam does not originate from the same source as in Christianity. Negative depictions of Jews in Islam tend to focus on the characteristic of humiliation. Some Islamic texts depict Jews as a humiliated group due to their perceived disobedience to God's law. Muhammad's own relationships with Jews are known to have been mixed. Muhammad was known to have had Jewish friends and one Jewish wife, who later converted to Islam, but also engaged in numerous battles with Jewish tribes (Poliakov, 1974: 41–43). Jewish defeats in such battles are commonly cited as an additional reason for Jews being viewed as a submissive, humiliated group (Lewis, 1999: 129–130). Therefore, while there are indeed strains of religious antisemitism in both Christianity and Islam, the sources and points of emphases tend to differ between these religious traditions—with Christian antisemitism focusing on deicide and blood libel and Islamic antisemitism focusing on humiliation and disobedience.

Economic Antisemitism

Economic antisemitism has its roots in medieval Europe, where Jews were often restricted to occupations considered socially inferior by Christians, such as tax collecting and moneylending. This was in large part due to Christian doctrine of the time that considered charging interest on loans to be sinful—a belief that continues in certain Islamic societies. One reason that Jews were allowed to engage in moneylending, although considered a sinful activity, was that Jews were already considered to be damned. Moreover, by Jews filling these occupations this would save the souls of Christians who would otherwise take on such roles (Todeschini, 2004: 11; Penslar, 2001: 18). This situation caused Jews to carry a stigma of being unproductive, parasitic, usurious, dishonest, dangerous, and so on (Schweitzer and Perry, 2002: 133).

By the eighteenth century, some estimate that as many as three-fourths of Jews in central and western Europe were involved in money-lending occupations (Sachar, 2005). Later, Jewish Emancipation in the nineteenth century allowed European Jews to engage in a wider variety of occupations, including law and medicine (Schweitzer and Perry, 2002: 136). Nonetheless, the medieval stigma of Jews as sinful, dishonest, and usurious continued and became the basis for a number of anti-semitic stereotypes and canards. These stereotypes tend to portray Jews as stingy, greedy, controlling, and wealthy. The canards often depict powerful Jews as having control over the business world and being a scapegoat for gentile hardship, such as in *The Protocols of the Elders of Zion,* an antisemitic hoax document that came out of Russia in 1903.

Remarkably, economic antisemitism has been used to accuse Jews of being responsible for the ills of both capitalism and communism. In fact, Karl Marx singled out Jews and claimed that since many worked in what he considered "non-productive" occupations, they could be blamed for a great deal of exploitation and alienation of workers (Schweitzer and Perry, 2002: 153–156). Marx even went so far as to argue that Jews embodied capitalism, because, according to him, Jewish culture shared elements of materialism and egoism that he also attributed to capitalism (Penslar, 2001). Marx wrote that, "Because of Judaism, money has become the essence of man's life and work . . . Jews are the embodiment of capitalism in action and the creators of all its evil consequences for humanity" (Schweitzer and Perry, 2002: 156). However, Jews have also been labeled as the driving force behind communism as well. During the Russian Civil War, the propaganda of the anticommunist "White" forces often tied Judaism and Bolshevism together and claimed that Jews were behind the communist movement in order to serve their own interests. This myth grew in large part due to the circulation of *The Protocols of the Elders of Zion* (Pipes, 1997: 93). Since that time, the notion of "Jewish Bolshevism" has been perpetuated as a conspiracy theory and has at times been viewed as a threat by nationalist factions in numerous countries.

While there is no single overriding myth with regard to economic antisemitism, there are a number of stereotypes that have endured and have provided the basis for various canards. The perception among many that Jews are stingy, greedy, dishonest, and unproductive has carried on since the medieval era. These characteristics have defined the numerous conspiracy theories that tend to scapegoat Jews for the hardships of gentiles. Jews have been blamed for the negative aspects of both capitalism and communism, which has allowed economic antisemitism to fester among many different ideologies and endure for centuries.

Racial Antisemitism

Racial antisemitism is distinct, in that it denotes prejudice or hatred of Jews as an ethnic group, rather than Judaism as a religion. Therefore, racial antisemitism purports that Jewish blood, and not simply Jewish beliefs, are inferior. Racial antisemitism is most commonly claimed to have originated in medieval Spain. During the Spanish Inquisition, many questioned the sincerity of those Jews who converted to Christianity (*conversos*). Consequently, an ideology of "cleanliness of blood" arose within the Spanish nobility, which influenced a series of statutes and legal decrees aimed at persecuting the conversos. Thus, the conversos could be persecuted based on their Jewish ancestry and ethnicity, rather than simply their beliefs (Kamen, 1998: 19–26; Murphy, 2012: 69–77).

Racial antisemitism increased in prominence in the nineteenth century due to a combination of increased popularity of nationalism and certain pseudoscientific theories such as eugenics. While neither ideology is inherently antisemitic, leaders adhering to these ideologies often embraced antisemitic racism as well. Francis Galton, often cited as the founder of modern eugenics, claimed that Jews were "specialized for a parasitical existence" (Pearson, 1924: 209). Such statements conveyed the notion that Jewish ethnicity predisposed one to particular behaviors and lifestyle. Galton was inspired by Charles Darwin's *On the Origin of Species* and developed eugenics as a means to improve human heredity. As the eugenics movement grew, various policies were proposed to coerce societies into producing what could be considered more "fit" children. Such policies first targeted the mentally and physically handicapped, but later came to include numerous other groups including Jews (Levy, 2005: 212).

Around the same time, romantic nationalism began to spread across Europe that relied upon the idea that a historic ethnic culture could lead a nation to a romantic ideal. The rise of such populist, *völkisch* movements was inspired not only by international events, such as the American and French revolutions, but also by the literature and philosophy of such figures as Johann Gottfried von Herder, the Brothers Grimm, Georg Wilhelm Friedrich Hegel, and Johann Gottlieb Fichte (Wilson, 1973: 828–830). Although these movements were not universally antisemitic, romantic nationalism often placed an emphasis on exclusivity, purity, and the superiority of one particular ethnic group over all others. Consequently, Jews were often viewed as an impediment or obstacle to a nation achieving its romantic ideal. For example, Richard Wagner claimed to identify "Jewishness" in musical style, due to what he asserted was Jews' unwillingness to assimilate into German culture and truly comprehend the nation's music and language (Wagner, 1869). Wagner did not claim that these perceived deficiencies were necessarily the result of Jewish beliefs, but rather saw them as an inherent quality of ethnic Jews. In these ways, romantic nationalism often allowed for Jews to not only be viewed as a scapegoat, but also as an impediment to the ambitions of a nation and ethnic culture to achieve an ideal.

When combined, pseudoscientific eugenics theory and romantic nationalism tend to reinforce one another with regard to their emphases on ethnic superiority and exclusivity. Although not necessarily based on antisemitic grounds, these ideologies became important contributors to the development of racial antisemitism. Both ideologies allowed for certain out-groups to be viewed as inferior, which Jews were often considered. However, with the rise of eugenics and romantic nationalism, Jewish inferiority could now not only be attributed to a particular belief system, but also a genetic predisposition. This is the primary way in which racial antisemitism differs from other forms.

Political Antisemitism

Political antisemitism shares many of the same traits associated with economic antisemitism, except the emphasis is placed on a different sector of society. Political antisemitism most often relies on conspiracy theories based on the belief that Jews seek national or world power and do so using illegitimate or criminal means. Because of such perceived Jewish ambitions, political antisemites often view Jews as an enemy and tend to place blame on Jews for their own political defeats. Such sentiment is often inflamed by international events, especially those relating to the Israeli-Palestinian conflict, and can occasionally translate into official antisemitic positions in political party platforms.

Although antisemitism and anti-Zionism are different phenomena, Holocaust denial has often served as a link between the two. In this way, Holocaust denial has become one of the more prominent expressions of political antisemitism. After World War II, some claimed that the Holocaust was part of a conspiracy—in that the genocide was either a hoax or the numbers were grossly inflated—in order to achieve Zionist objectives (Martin, 2015: 138). These claims asserted that Zionists either imagined, exaggerated, or were even complicit in the Holocaust in order to gain greater leverage in negotiations with Western powers for the establishment of a Jewish state (Herf, 2013; Wistrich, 2012). Similar accusations of Zionist conspiracies have been leveled to deny, minimize, or in some cases justify other violent acts committed against Jews, including the October 7, 2023, Hamas attacks on Israeli civilians. Some contemporary radical political figures contend that Zionists/Jews continue to yield illegitimate influence in Western governments, in part due to what they consider the leverage gained through mythical or exaggerated understandings of the Holocaust and its aftermath (Liang, 2013: 158).

These sorts of suspicions and fears have become a central element in the ideologies and doctrines of numerous antisemitic political parties and movements. Notably, antisemitism is not exclusive to any particular end of the political spectrum. Rather, Jewish motifs are often used to represent an enemy from many different directions (Gross, 2007). This phenomenon is vividly demonstrated throughout Russian history, where Jews faced persecution from both communist and anticommunist factions (Korey, 1995). One crucial factor in developing group unity in any political movement is defining an enemy to mobilize against. And given their distinct history, culture, and religious beliefs, Jews have consequently been perceived in many cases as outsiders, even in countries in which they may have resided for generations. Propaganda plays an important role in identifying, isolating, and excluding these "outsider" groups. By defining the enemy in this manner, it becomes easier for parties or movements to air grievances against the particular enemy or "out-group" and scapegoat them for hardships and setbacks (Arendt,

1951: 43–47). The sources of grievances and scapegoating may differ between regions and parties; however, the tactic of defining Jews as an enemy to rally against and consequently strengthen group unity is a common theme in political antisemitism.

A Renewed Definition

To better reflect the manifestations outlined in this chapter, I will use the following operational definition of *antisemitism* throughout this analysis: *hostile attitudes or attacks targeting Jewish people, symbols, or interests based on religious, economic, racial, or political grounds.*

This definition refers to "hostile attitudes or attacks" because these are important indicators, which are most typically used in measuring levels of antisemitism. The definition refers to "targeting Jewish people, symbols, or interests" because these are easily identifiable, tangible things against which hateful, discriminatory attitudes or attacks are most often aimed. And finally, this definition notes that these attitudes or attacks are based on "religious, economic, racial, or political grounds" to emphasize the different manifestations of antisemitism. For these reasons, this definition best and most concisely encompasses the ways in which antisemitism is measured and tends to manifest itself.

Working Toward Solutions

Although antisemitic hatred dates back thousands of years, many of the strategies designed to combat it have only been implemented since the end of the Cold War, and many within the past ten to twenty years. Therefore, it has only recently become possible to thoroughly analyze these approaches and the consequent effects on the groups and individuals that they concern. This research will contribute to our understanding of the strategies implemented and analyze which have been most effective in reducing levels of antisemitism—valuable information for scholars, government officials, and nongovernmental organizations.

While research on the problem of European antisemitism in the twentieth century is quite abundant, there is need for a study examining antisemitism in the twenty-first century and the contemporary strategies meant to combat it. In this book, I seek to fill this void and advance our understanding of the issue with three pressing areas of examination.

First, much of the existing literature on antisemitism needs updating due to the changing demographics and political dynamics of Europe in the twenty-first century. While previous works have explored the ideologies of far-right, far-left, and Islamist groups that often share antisemitic views dating back before the Holocaust and through the Cold War, there are few studies that have examined these groups and their evolution into the twenty-first century. This book provides extensive detail on the historical manifestations of antisemitism and goes a step further by examining how these historical roots have shaped contemporary antisemitic movements and ideologies.

Second, beyond simply examining the nature of antisemitism it is also crucial to develop a better understanding of the strategies in place to counter the problem. To date, there has not been a comprehensive work that has clearly defined and examined both the nature of antisemitism as well as the strategies to combat it. This book will work to accomplish just that.

Currently, there are two primary methods to address this problem—antiradicalization legal measures and public diplomacy. Although Germany and Poland have minimal coordination in their efforts, both use these two methods as the primary means of countering antisemitism. The legal measures tend to be more focused on punishing certain acts, such as Holocaust denial, spreading antisemitic propaganda, or hate crimes. On the other hand, public diplomacy initiatives attempt to influence perceptions and attitudes. Comparing the strategies of these two countries and analyzing the results will enable an evaluation of which approaches tend to achieve the most desirable outcomes and where holes exist in the current strategies.

While the legal measures may well be understood through an examination of legislation and government institutions, *public diplomacy* is a more complex term that has not been as clearly defined by the existing literature. Public diplomacy is a term most commonly used to describe communication from one country to foreign audiences; however, antisemitism is a unique issue in which public diplomacy initiatives have been launched to specifically address a domestic problem. Most conceptions of public diplomacy tend to focus on the idea of "promotion" and emphasizing the positive aspects of a country's culture, political values, and foreign policies, but these conceptions do not adequately address such a situation in which public diplomacy is connected so closely to a domestic problem. These two central European countries have been rare cases where public diplomacy has been employed to listen to controversial and negative perceptions, which have consequently motivated domestic reforms. A primary reason for this is that antisemitism uniquely affects both foreign perceptions of a country's identity and its domestic environment. A major contribution of this work is the reframing of what public diplomacy is, as well as how it can be used to work toward reconciliation and rehabilitation for societies marked by traumatic events such as genocide.

Third, understanding the strengths and weaknesses of the current strategies to counter antisemitism is essential to improving approaches going forward. The data most important to this study is data collected over time so that we may assess the effectiveness of strategies since their implementation. This book presents data on such indicators as antisemitic groups, crimes, and attitudes in each case in order to evaluate the effectiveness of the current strategies in place. The later chapters of the book will evaluate such data from a variety of governmental and nongovernmental sources to provide a comprehensive picture of the contemporary situation. This analysis will assist in determining which areas current strategies tend to be most and least effective in order to improve them moving forward.

Composition and Structure of the Book

While the focus of this book is on contemporary antisemitism, it is impossible to fully comprehend the problem without a deep understanding of the historical roots that have led to this point. Antisemitism has evolved over millennia and consequently has manifested itself in a variety of ways. Chapters 2 and 3 will flesh out these manifestations as they relate to the cases of Germany and Poland. In these chapters, I will examine the chronology of how the primary manifestations of antisemitism have developed and become part of the contemporary problem in each case.

Chapters 4 and 5 will examine the strategies that have been employed in Germany and Poland to respond to the problem of antisemitism, primarily since the end of the Cold War. As such, these chapters will include a discussion of the laws and public diplomacy initiatives that have been implemented in each country. This discussion will be informed by a detailed analysis of the governmental and nongovernmental institutions tasked with leading and implementing the approach. Special attention will be paid to the ways in which the respective governments and civil societies have attempted to connect their approaches with problems specific to their country.

Chapters 6 and 7 will present data and detailed explanations of contemporary antisemitism in Germany and Poland focusing on the period since 1990. The main goal of these chapters will be to evaluate the successes and failures of the strategies to counter antisemitism in each country. To accomplish this, I will present and analyze the data relevant to each case over time. This will require a thorough analysis of the effects that the approaches have had on different antisemitic groups, attitudes, and crimes. These chapters will also examine the welfare and perceptions of the domestic Jewish community in each country.

Finally, Chapter 8 will analyze the major findings of the study and provide concise answers to the central research questions. In doing so, the chapter will detail the major themes and patterns of this research and their practical implications, which will be used to provide recommendations for policymaking in the future. I will close the chapter by suggesting some potential avenues for further research.

The overarching goal of this book is to provide a deeper understanding of antisemitism and how to combat it. Antisemitic beliefs are some of the most difficult to counter, given that they have persisted since antiquity and continue to motivate conspiracy theories, harassment, and violent attacks in modern times. These concerns are heightened in the cases presented in this book because Germany and Poland remain marked by the legacy of the Holocaust. Addressing the horrors of genocide remains a major challenge for both countries, domestically and internationally. These dynamics provide increased motivation for both countries to counter the problem of antisemitism and work toward reconciliation. Of course, antisemitism and the legacies of genocide and ethnic and religious hatred are not exclusive to these two cases. Therefore, by accomplishing its primary goal, this book will provide answers to questions that not only establish a better understanding of working toward reconciliation and countering hatred in central Europe, but also provide lessons applicable to other regions that have been scarred by hatred and traumatic historical events.

Notes

1. One of the most discussed and widely used definitions of *antisemitism* comes from the International Holocaust Remembrance Alliance (IHRA). Its definition is as follows: "Antisemitism is a certain perception of Jews, which may be expressed as hatred toward Jews. Rhetorical and physical manifestations of antisemitism are directed toward Jewish or non-Jewish individuals and/or their property, toward Jewish community institutions and religious facilities" (International Holocaust Remembrance Alliance, 2023). This definition is followed by eleven examples, seven of which relate to the State of Israel. This latter part in particular has made the definition controversial, as critics view it as stifling critiques of the Israeli government. I

believe one flaw with the definition is that while it alludes to manifestations of anti-semitism, it does not explicitly state what those are, which is part of the reason for controversy and also limits the definition's utility. Another common definition is known as the Jerusalem Declaration on Antisemitism. This alternative definition is a concise sixteen words and reads as follows: "Antisemitism is discrimination, preju-dice, hostility or violence against Jews as Jews (or Jewish institutions as Jewish)" (Jerusalem Declaration on Antisemitism, 2023). While this definition is concise, it is also quite vague and, like the IHRA definition, does not address the manifestations from which the hatred originates. Due to these shortcomings, I have developed my own operational definition, presented in Chapter 1, which concisely states how anti-semitism manifests itself and is most commonly measured.

2

Antisemitism in Germany

BY EXPLAINING THE ROOTS OF ANTISEMITISM, THIS CHAPTER WILL LAY THE foundation for better understanding the data and nature of contemporary antisemitism addressed in subsequent chapters. The examination of the historical development and modern manifestations of antisemitism in Germany begins with the development of religious antisemitism—the oldest manifestation—and includes the influence of accusations of deicide and blood libel, derogatory Christian depictions of Jews stemming from the Middle Ages, the Nazi revival of such myths and depictions, and antisemitism within Germany's growing Muslim community. From there, I go on to explore the development of economic, racial, and political antisemitism.

Religious Antisemitism in Germany

The earliest known Jewish settlements on the land that forms modern Germany were most likely established around the fourth century—coinciding with Christianity becoming the state religion of the Roman Empire (Lieu, North, and Rajak, 2013: 117). This time period was marked by increased hostility toward Jews, with such hostility often based on religious grounds. Once Christianity became the state religion of Rome, Jews became targeted for attack more frequently and experienced greater restrictions on their political rights. Many of these measures and other attacks on Jewish people, symbols, and interests have been attributed to hostility in early Christian literature related to claims of collective Jewish responsibility for Jesus's execution (Schweitzer and Perry, 2002: 26). These claims were based on passages in the New Testament, in particular Matthew 27:24–25, in which Jews shout that Jesus's blood is on their and their children's hands. In addition, the first Christian emperor of Rome, Constantine I, instituted a number of policies regulating Jewish religious services, restricting congregations, outlawing Christian conversion to Judaism, and banning intermarriage between Christians and unconverted Jews (Cohn-Sherbok, 2006: 34–35). Due to these factors, one may claim that the religious strain of antisemitism has existed on German land for as long as the Jewish communities that settled there.

Over the following centuries, Jewish communities continued to expand on German lands, although the civic and social status of Jews varied across the subsequently established Germanic kingdoms. The situation worsened significantly, however, around the time of the First Crusade in 1096. In fact, German Jews were one of the first groups persecuted as part of the Crusades. Jewish communities tended to be in much closer proximity to Catholic communities in central Europe than the more distant Muslims. And since Jews continued to be blamed by many for the death of Christ, they were often viewed as just as much an enemy as Muslims. The Frankish knight Godfrey of Bouillon, one of the leaders of the German Crusade, demonstrated the religious antisemitism of the time by vowing "to go on this journey only after avenging the blood of the crucified one by shedding Jewish blood and completely eradicating any trace of those bearing the name 'Jew,' thus assuaging his own burning wrath" (Eidelberg, 1977: 25). This type of sentiment led to massacres of Jews in the Rhineland, with an estimated 12,000 executed in the summer of 1096 alone. The entire Jewish communities in Cologne, Worms, Trier, and Mainz were eradicated during this time (Riley-Smith, 1991). In other areas where many of the native Jews survived, these Jews were nonetheless frequently the targets of extortion by crusaders seeking to supply themselves on their mission (Golb, 1998). Other Jews, such as those in the city of Regensburg, were subjected to involuntary mass baptisms in the Danube (Baron, 1957). The Crusades led to one of the widest-scale and most-aggressive persecutions of German Jews prior to the Holocaust. However, whereas many future persecutions were often the result of a culmination of strains of antisemitism, the persecution during the Crusades was defined primarily by an intensely religious antisemitism.

Religious antisemitism continued to be perpetuated throughout the Middle Ages, often through imagery depicting Jews in derogatory or dehumanizing ways. These sorts of derogatory depictions of Jews were often part of imagery known as *Judensau* (Jews' sow) that portrayed Jews in obscene positions with unclean animals and often added elements of Jews representing the devil. *Judensau* imagery began to appear in the thirteenth century and even appeared on church or cathedral walls in the centuries following (Schreckenburg, 1996: 331–337). These sorts of depictions of Jews worked to reinforce the portrayal of the Jew as a Christ killer and became a clear manifestation of religious antisemitism. Some of the most notable examples of *Judensau* appear on churches in the city of Wittenberg, including on the façade of the Stadtkirche where Martin Luther preached (Wolffsohn, 1993: 194). *Judensau* remained popular in many of the German territories until the nineteenth century and became one of the most visible manifestations of religious antisemitism that reinforced and perpetuated a number of Christian suspicions and myths regarding Jews and their religious practices. Despite legal challenges arguing that the depictions are defamatory toward Jews, *Judensau* sculptures, drawings, and carvings remain on numerous German churches due to court rulings, which have stated that the images do not violate existing law (Chambers, 2022).

A frequent lack of Christian understanding and tolerance for Jews and their religious practices also manifested itself in various accusations leveled against Jews for events that, at the time, many believed could not be otherwise explained. Jews often became the scapegoats for such things as outbreaks of disease and cases of missing and deceased children. Throughout the Middle Ages, populations often lacked basic understanding of how diseases spread, and this tended to lead survivors to search for reasons why crowded cities could experience massive outbreaks of illness. A common scapegoat for these outbreaks of disease were city-dwelling Jews, who often lived in segregated ghettos and became accused of poisoning the wells. The widest known persecutions due to such accusations were during the bubonic plague, including in the German city of Erfurt where estimates suggest anywhere from a few hundred to 3,000 Jews were executed based on well-poisoning accusations (Laqueur, 2006: 62). Blood libel, the false accusation that Jews murder Christian children in order to use their blood in religious rituals, was also commonly invoked as an explanation for children who went missing and were subsequently found dead (Aring, 1998: 837–838). There were about 150 recorded cases of blood libel, with thousands of other rumors, around Europe throughout the Middle Ages that led to the revenge killings and persecutions of Jews for centuries (Laqueur, 2006: 56).

Through the Age of Enlightenment, many Jews continued to lack certain civil and social rights; however, the degree of violent attacks and persecutions was not on par with the levels experienced during the Middle Ages. In fact, a number of Jews, such as Moses Mendelsohn, were able to increase their social standing and civic enfranchisement during the Enlightenment by influencing German thought and scholarship. The Jewish Reform movement also served to better integrate many Jews into German society. During the nineteenth century, Jewish life often vacillated between periods of freedom and of oppression, with Jews receiving ostensible legal equality following the revolutions of 1848 (Johnson, 1988: 395). From the late nineteenth to early twentieth century, religious antisemitism had largely given way to other strains of antisemitism that began to rise around this time.

The rise of the Nazis during the 1920s and 1930s caused a revival of the rhetoric and many of the themes associated with religious antisemitism that had been so influential in Jewish persecutions centuries earlier. Many scholars argue that the strain of religious antisemitism tracing back centuries played a pivotal role in conditioning many Germans to accept Jewish persecution. For this reason, the Nazis often invoked the writings of Martin Luther to expand the appeal of their policies and justify their approach to certain audiences. The most prominent of Luther's writings distributed by the Nazis was his treatise entitled *On the Jews and Their Lies*, which was known to have been distributed at the Nuremberg rallies and passages of which were published in the Nazi newspaper *Der Stürmer* (Ellis, 2004). Passages such as these reinforced the Nazi argument for the extermination of Jews and added a religious aspect to the other forms of antisemitism exhibited by the regime.

Although Nazism itself was not an inherently religious movement, elements of German society did indeed attempt to align Christianity with Nazi beliefs more closely. The most prominent Nazi-aligned religious movement was the German Christians (Deutsche Christen), who can most concisely be described as a group of nationalist, Nazi Protestants. The German Christians actively promoted many of Luther's antisemitic writings and attempted to transform Christian theology to also reflect Nazi ideals. Consequently, this particular religious faction sought to de-emphasize the Old Testament in Protestantism and remove portions of the Bible that were deemed to be "too Jewish" (Bergen, 1996). The Nazi Party encouraged these sorts of beliefs through what was termed "positive Christianity," which blended ideas of racial purity and Nazi ideology with elements of Christian theology. Adolf Hitler even claimed in a March 23, 1933, speech to the Reichstag that Christianity was the "foundation" of German values (US Holocaust Memorial Museum, 2023a). Many historians, however, such as Ian Kershaw and Laurence Rees, argue that Hitler did not necessarily have much regard for faith and religion, but rather used religion pragmatically due to its historical importance and influence in German society (Rees, 2012: 135). So, while Nazism itself was not necessarily based in theology, in practice the Nazi Party was opportunistic in using religion to strengthen support for its antisemitic policies.

Following World War II and the Holocaust, the strain of religious antisemitism became less prominent within Germany, although the symbolism and rhetoric of modern antisemitism often reflects some similar themes. Religion in general has declined in Germany, in part due to the imposition of communism in the eastern portion of the country during the Cold War and moves toward secularism in parts of the west. In fact, a 2006 survey showed that 51 percent of German youth between the ages of twelve and twenty-four were either agnostic or atheist (Gensicke, 2007). Such data suggests that religious antisemitism likely does not have the same levels of resonance as it once did, for example, during the Middle Ages or the Reformation. Christian churches have also become more likely to actively denounce antisemitic behavior, with events such as the Second Vatican Council aiming, in part, to repair relations between Christians and Jews and repudiate particular sources of religious antisemitism, such as allegations of deicide. Many in the Lutheran Church have also come to renounce the more antisemitic writings of the church's founder. Nonetheless, certain rhetoric, such as the common antisemitic slur *Judenschwein* (Jewish pig), originate from the religious strain of antisemitism that has existed for centuries. Synagogues also remain one of the prime targets of antisemitic attacks, with the German government reporting eighty-two attacks on synagogues between 2008 and 2012 (*Times of Israel,* 2013). So, while there has been some movement on improving Christian-Jewish relations in recent years, there are indeed elements of modern antisemitism in Germany that mirror the sort of religiously based attacks that have taken place for centuries.

At the same time, Germany has experienced a surge in its Muslim population since the end of World War II, and this has made Islamic-Jewish relations an increasingly important dynamic in the study of antisemitism within the country. By 2006, Muslims were estimated to make up approximately 5 percent of the total German population. Germany's Muslim population is also markedly more religious than the non-Muslim population, with a 2006 survey showing that 73 percent of German Muslims claimed to be either "fairly religious" or "very religious" compared to less than 30 percent for non-Muslims (Gesemann, 2006: 8–9). There is some evidence of Islamic religious antisemitism in Germany— particularly with regard to the belief that Jews are to be a subject of ridicule—with a 2012 survey of Turkish-German Muslims showing that 18 percent believed Jews to be inferior human beings (*Die Welt*, 2012). However, while there does indeed appear to be some traces of religious antisemitism among Germany's Muslim population, other manifestations tend to be more prominent in the contemporary environment.

Economic Antisemitism in Germany

In Germany, economic antisemitism was in part borne out of religious antisemitism but has nonetheless become its own distinct form over time. Following the First Crusade, Jews were frequently subjected to various legal restrictions, many of which centered on the types of occupations that they could fill. Occupations such as moneylending and tax collecting tended to be viewed as socially inferior; in fact, moneylending with interest was considered sinful by Catholic doctrine throughout the Middle Ages. Whether by choice or necessity, these occupations were often filled by Jews and consequently led to a number of stereotypes and adversarial relationships that have come to characterize the essence of economic antisemitism.

As many Jews entered financial occupations, the relationships between Christians and Jews often became more adversarial, with Christian debtors viewing Jewish creditors as greedy usurers (Dimont, 2004: 268). A number of rulers throughout the Holy Roman Empire relied on Jewish financiers, commonly referred to as Court Jews, to negotiate financial agreements and ensure that their territories had a requisite number of resources. Given their influence and social connections in such positions, Court Jews would frequently make a number of enemies—enemies who would occasionally target the Court Jews following the death of the ruler for whom they had worked (Tegel, 2011). This phenomenon was reflected in an iconic piece of German literature and film known by the name *Jud Süß* (Süss the Jew). Many adaptations of *Jud Süß* were not intended to have antisemitic undertones; however, the story of *Jud Süß* came to reinforce a number of economic stereotypes regarding Jews and indeed became an influential part of Nazi propaganda through film. *Jud Süß* became a figure representing the stigma of Jews as usurious, manipulative, and fraudulent financiers—thus serving as a prime representation of economic antisemitism that has carried on for centuries.

During the nineteenth century, Jews in a number of German territories such as Prussia, Hesse, Württemberg, and Hanover had been emancipated as citizens, were granted new civil rights, and were able to elevate their social standing. The establishment of the German Empire in 1871 also removed many of the remaining legal barriers that Jews had faced. This allowed many German Jews to become more influential in fields previously not available to them, such as literature, politics, and law. However, while a number of legal barriers were indeed lifted, manifestations of economic antisemitism remained (Lazare, 1903). The perceptions of Jews as powerful and rich were often exacerbated via literature and theater at the time with figures such as the Rothschild family often depicted to be, as Howard Sachar describes, "Jewish cash bags" or "Jews behind the throne" (Sachar, 2005). While many of these works were intended as satire, they were in many cases consistent with the sort of stereotypes and perceptions associated with economic antisemitism that gained momentum in the decades that followed.

During the beginning of the twentieth century, Jews became increasingly integrated within German society, so much so that a higher percentage of German Jews fought in World War I than any other religious or ethnic group in Germany (Rigg, 2002: 72). In the Weimar Republic, many Jews began to play a major role in politics and diplomacy and were able to achieve greater social status than was previously possible. In fact, Hugo Preuß, the Weimar Republic's first interior minister, authored the initial draft of the Weimar Constitution (Stirk, 2002). Nonetheless, antisemitic beliefs continued to manifest themselves. In the early 1920s, there were sporadic outbreaks of antisemitism, with some claiming that Jews betrayed Germany and were responsible for defeat in World War I—a myth known as the *Dolchstoßlegende* (Stab-in-the-back myth). *The Protocols of the Elders of Zion* was first published in German in 1920, leading to wider dissemination of conspiracy theories targeting Jews. The anticommunist, and increasingly antisemitic, Freikorps paramilitary organization also became more active during this period. Although there were clear examples of antisemitism throughout the 1920s that often scapegoated Jews and alleged various conspiracy theories, the consequent violence tended to be sporadic rather than systematic. However, once economic circumstances changed in 1929 with the onset of the Great Depression, antipathy toward Jews increased rapidly and antisemitism became more systematic than at any other time in history.

The Nazi regime embodied each major strain of antisemitism, but one must note that the Nazi rise to power occurred in an environment of economic depression. The late 1920s and 1930s was certainly a time of economic anxiety and despair within Germany due to economic decline, rapid monetary inflation, and the onset of the Great Depression. Hitler directly pinned blame for such circumstances on German Jews and on what he argued were Jewish attempts to bolshevize Germany. The following passage from *Mein Kampf* is a prime example of such sentiments:

> The Jewish train of thought in all this is clear. The Bolshevization of Germany—that is, the extermination of the national folkish Jewish intelligentsia to make possible the sweating of the German working class under the yoke of Jewish world finance—is conceived only as a preliminary to the further extension of this Jewish tendency of world conquest. . . . If our people and our state become the victim of these blood-thirsty and avaricious Jewish tyrants of nations, the whole earth will sink into the snares of this octopus. (Downs, 2004: 361)

These sorts of conspiracy theories gained traction during the Nazi regime and played a key role in the justification for the passage of the Nuremberg Laws and the boycotting of Jewish shops and services. In fact, the Nazi-led boycott of Jewish businesses was one of the first measures taken by Hitler after his appointment as chancellor—taking office on January 30, 1933, and beginning the boycott on April 1, 1933 (Lang, 2009: 132). As state efforts against Jewish business progressed, harassment, vandalism, arrests, and pillaging became increasingly common, with November 9–10, 1938—known as *Kristallnacht* (Night of Broken Glass)—being the most vivid example. Jews were also increasingly segregated from Aryan Germans and were eventually banned from public schools, universities, cinemas, theaters, and other recreational facilities. Such restrictions had devastating impacts on Jewish economic and professional life. Of the 50,000 businesses in Berlin in 1939, all had Aryan owners by 1945 (Kreutzmüller, 2012). Economic antisemitism was indeed visible from the earliest days of the Nazi regime and was one of the primary means of separating Jews from the rest of the German population.

Given that Germany's Jewish population had been devastated and greatly reduced due to the Holocaust, the effects of economic anti-semitism were less pronounced in the postwar period but did nonetheless exist to varying extents in the German Democratic Republic (GDR) and the Federal Republic of Germany (FRG). A primary economic motivation that fueled resentment against Germany's remaining Jewish community was the notion of restitution and reparations for those Jews who had their property confiscated following the rise of the Nazi government in 1933. Legislation drafted by the Allied countries obligated German property owners to return property confiscated from Jews after 1933 to the original owners or their heirs. Such laws were criticized by many Germans and led to bitter fights between German and Jewish property owners. The press, particularly in the FRG, often criticized such policies and portrayed them as unjust (Bergmann and Erb, 1997: 13). Also in the FRG, Germans who were compelled to return property formed various organizations that often focused on the most controversial aspects of the restitution procedures and perpetuated negative economic stereotypes of Jews. Many of the publications of such organizations selected particular cases to portray the surviving Jews as corrupt and in pursuit of personal enrichment. While these efforts were primarily intended to pressure the federal government to revise, or completely end, the restitution policies, they also served as a prominent manifestation of antisemitism in the post–World War II period (Bergmann and Erb, 1997: 13).

It is important to note that while there is insufficient data to effectively compare antisemitic attitudes in the FRG and GDR from 1945–1990, the Jewish populations in both states varied significantly. According to the 1933 census, pre–World War II Germany had an estimated Jewish population of 500,000. By 1945, the FRG had approximately 37,000 Jews, while the GDR only had a few hundred. These numbers decreased even further in the decades following the war, as many Jews emigrated to Israel, the United States, Canada, the United Kingdom, and other locations (US Holocaust Memorial Museum, 2023c). So, while the FRG had a greatly decreased Jewish population, the GDR had a virtual absence of Jews. As there were no extensive surveys conducted on antisemitic attitudes in the former GDR, it is difficult to compare the attitudes between the separate German states before 1990.

Nonetheless, surveys conducted in the FRG indicate that the economic discrimination and boycotts of Jewish businesses had a lingering effect in the postwar period. Negative stereotypes of Jews remained relatively consistent during the period of a divided Germany, with 23 percent of West Germans agreeing in 1960/1961 that "greedy" was a "Jewish characteristic" and 20 percent still holding such a view in 1986/1987 (Bergmann and Erb, 1997: 111). Such attitudes were also reflected in attitudes toward Jewish-owned businesses. In 1949, 25 percent of West Germans rejected the idea of shopping in Jewish-owned stores, even if the prices were lower. Notably, this sort of economic antisemitism was more prevalent among the well-educated, of whom 30 percent responded that they would avoid Jewish stores, compared to 22 percent of those with only an elementary education. Surveys taken in 1961 and 1965 also demonstrated that 14 percent of West Germans had reservations about being treated by a Jewish doctor. West German women were more likely to have such reservations than men—18 percent compared to 10 percent. These gender-specific differences are most likely due to Nazi stereotypes that depicted Jewish men as sexually aggressive and condemned any contact between Jews and other Germans (Bergmann and Erb, 1997: 150–151). So, while the Nazi regime may have ended in 1945, the legacy of economic discrimination and stereotypes remained among about a quarter of the West German population in the decades following World War II.

Shortly after German reunification, it became possible to compare data on antisemitism in the states that composed the former GDR and the FRG. Notably, eastern Germans tended to feel less threatened by Jewish influence than their counterparts in the areas of western Germany. In 1994, only 8 percent of East Germans agreed with the statement that "Jews have too much influence in our society," whereas 24 percent of West Germans agreed with such a statement (Weil, 1997: 114). Of course, the responses to this statement may be influenced by the higher Jewish population in West Germany and the relative homogeneity of the former East.

However, while such antisemitic attitudes may have been less prevalent in the former East, the fervency of those with such beliefs and the propensity for violence tended to be higher on average in the eastern states. In response to a question as to whether or not a respondent believes "antisemitic groups have a big following," 36 percent of former East Germans answered yes, whereas only 26 percent of West Germans responded similarly (Weil, 1997: 119). Furthermore, between 1991 and 1995, about one-third of violent hate crimes in Germany occurred in the former East, which, relative to population, means that such crimes were on average more likely to occur in the eastern states (Bergmann, 1997: 34). These data indicate that while antisemitic attitudes may have been higher in the western states, those with antisemitic beliefs in the eastern states tended to be more likely to join organizations and act on such beliefs.

Fueled by conspiracy theories and scapegoating, economic antisemitism has long remained a problem in German society. In many ways, economic antisemitism has its roots in religious antisemitism, and indeed these two strains have often paralleled one another throughout history. Many of the negative Christian depictions of Jews as untrustworthy and conniving for their alleged role as conspirators in the death of Christ parallel the images of Jews with regard to economic problems. In many different periods of German history, policies were implemented to restrict economic opportunities for Jews and constrain them to certain professions. These restrictions consequently created many of the stereotypes and prejudices that persist. In these ways, economic antisemitism has contributed to and continues to fuel the problem of antisemitism in Germany.

Racial Antisemitism in Germany

Racial antisemitism differs from other forms in that hostility is instead based on racial or ethnic grounds. The rise of racial antisemitism in Germany is most commonly attributed to two main factors: pseudo-sciences (e.g., eugenics) and ethnic nationalism (Ehrenreich, 2007: 135). Whereas religious antisemitism commonly pinned blame on Jews for deicide and economic antisemitism pinned blame on Jews for various economic problems, racial antisemitism tended to pin blame on Jews for preventing the majority race from reaching a national ideal. In Germany, racial antisemitism largely arose from the romantic nationalism of the nineteenth century and culminated during the Nazi era. Given the emphasis on genetics and purity of blood that racial antisemitism often emphasizes, Jews are commonly viewed by racial antisemites to be essentially incurable. This rationale is often cited as a primary motivation for the mass extermination of the Jewish race and is therefore arguably the most dangerous and potentially violent manifestation of antisemitism (Ehrenreich, 2007: 175).

While the origins of racial antisemitism can be found in the history of the Spanish Inquisition, this strain of antisemitism did not become a significant factor in Germany until the rise of romantic nationalism in the nineteenth century. An important aspect of the romantic nationalism that began to arise in the early nineteenth century was the emergence of *völkisch* movements, which were often ethno-nationalist in nature. The German word *Volk* corresponds to the English word *people*; however, as used in this historical context, *Volk* tends to carry certain populist, ethnic connotations. As historian James Webb writes, the term *Volk* has at times carried "overtones of 'nation,' 'race,' and 'tribe'" articulated in an emotional tone (1976: 277; Pietikäinen, 2000: 524). These emotional elements often focused on the relationship between ethnicity and territory, with certain messages amplified through German folklore, local history, and anti-urban populism. Many of the *völkisch* movements, and romantic nationalism in general, emphasized ideas about nature and a certain natural order that created ideal images of society often based on ethnic homogeneity and superiority, and consequently subjugated the position and value of those perceived as outsiders.

Complementing this rise in ethnonationalist, *völkisch* movements was the emergence of racialized pseudosciences, such as eugenics, that focused on measures that some believed would improve the genetic quality of humanity. While eugenics began in England with the writings of Francis Galton, similar beliefs spread across Europe by other theorists, such as Arthur de Gobineau in France, who argued that the mixing of races caused a degeneration of humanity. He contended that whereas European civilization had once flowed from Greece to Rome, contemporary civilization was based in Germany, and that the German race was the most superior. He argued that contemporary German society corresponded to the ancient Indo-European culture and thus began using the term "Aryan" as synonymous with "German" (Bartulin, 2013: 23). However, de Gobineau asserted that just as past civilizations fell, German civilization would also fall once the races became "polluted," as he believed had already been the case in France.

While racial antisemitism had been ingrained within particular movements and pseudoscientific theories as far back as the early nineteenth century, this particular strain of antisemitism did not become a wide-scale public policy initiative in Germany until the rise of the Nazi Party in the 1930s. The belief that Jews as a race, and not merely a religion, were inherently inclined to subvert and poison society has arguably been the most important rationale for the oppression and genocide of Jews since the Middle Ages. The concept of "cleanliness of blood" that first arose during the Spanish Inquisition, and later became an important theme in Nazi propaganda, essentially did not allow for Jews to be "cured" of their Jewishness through means such as conversion and thus they were unable to function and participate fully as members of society. The Nazi movement built upon the racialist theories and ethnic nationalism of the nineteenth century and used such beliefs to develop and implement doctrines seeking to "purify" the blood of those in German society by diminishing the influence of, and eventually eliminating, the populations of those deemed undesirable and racially inferior.

One of the earliest, and most prominent, manifestations of Nazi racial antisemitism was the passage of the Nuremberg Laws that, among other things, forbade marriage or extramarital intercourse between Germans and Jews, forbade German females under forty-five years of age from working in Jewish households, and established that only those with German or related blood were eligible to be citizens of the Reich. The basis for such laws stemmed from the ideology of de Gobineau's belief that the mixing of races was a direct cause for the degeneration of humanity. Such thinking indeed became a cornerstone of Nazi ideology and policymaking, and the Nuremberg Laws provide a vivid example of the Nazi conception of race and the role of the state in preserving the purity of blood of the "superior" racial class.

Although the Nazi movement certainly invoked aspects of religious and economic antisemitism, racial antisemitism tended to be the strain most responsible for the massive scale of violence in the Third Reich. The concept of "racial hygiene" became a central part of both Nazi policy and propaganda and was a primary justification for the extermination of those races viewed as inferior or subhuman. While religious and economic antisemitism were commonly based upon certain grievances against a particular group, racial antisemitism placed particular values on racial groups as human beings—consequently deeming some more worthy of life than others. Propaganda and the spread of racially discriminatory messages were central to allowing policies of violence and mass extermination to be carried out to the levels that they were. Klaus Voegel, the director of Dresden's German Hygiene Museum, which played an important role in spreading racial propaganda, has stated that, "The Hygiene Museum was not a criminal institute in the sense that people were killed here, but it helped shape the idea of which lives were worthy and which were worthless" (Rietschel, 2006). Once again, unlike with religious or economic antisemitism, individual Jews cannot overcome hatred and discrimination through means such as conversion or good deeds in the minds of those who subscribe fully to racially antisemitic ideology.

As is the case with other manifestations of antisemitism, data suggest that elements of racial antisemitism existed within Germany even after the conclusion of World War II and the demise of the Nazi Party. For example, in 1946, a plurality of West Germans answered "yes" to the question "Do you think Nazism was a good idea that was badly implemented?"—47 percent answering "yes" and 41 percent answering "no." In fact, over the course of the following decade the percentage of those answering "yes" even increased: 55 percent in 1947/1948, 57 percent in 1948, and 55 percent in 1969. Those numbers eventually decreased over time, with 26 percent answering "yes" in 1977, 36 percent in 1979, and 26 percent in 1994 (Bergmann and Erb, 1997: 247).

Indeed, the ethno-nationalism, and particularly the antisemitic elements, was evident in other surveys as well. When asked "Would you say it would be better for Germany if there were no Jews in the country?"— 37 percent answered "yes" in 1952, 26 percent in 1956, 22 percent in 1958, 18 percent in 1963, 19 percent in 1965, 9 percent in 1983, 13 percent in 1987, and 18 percent in 1992 (Bergmann and Erb, 1997: 139). While the data indicate that these sorts of ethno-nationalist, antisemitic beliefs have generally declined over time, the data also indicate that the legacy of ethno-nationalist, racial antisemitism persisted in the decades following the fall of the Third Reich.

The combination of ethnic nationalism and pseudoscientific racial theories that originated in the nineteenth century were indeed predecessors to the Nazi ideology that endorsed genocide as policy. Data in the decades following World War II suggest that the influence of racial antisemitism continued even after the fall of the Nazi regime, so while the government may have fallen, the racially antisemitic propaganda and indoctrination had left a legacy that persisted in the following decades.

Political Antisemitism in Germany

Political antisemitism is closely related to economic antisemitism; however, political antisemitism often cites Zionism as the basis for numerous conspiracy theories. Consequently, political antisemitism is the most recent manifestation to arise in German society. Theodor Herzl, commonly viewed as the founder of modern political Zionism, first published his pamphlet entitled *Der Judenstaat* (The Jewish State) in 1896, which outlined the rationale and philosophy behind the creation of a Jewish state. Herzl's work was indeed controversial and was followed shortly by numerous works critiquing his philosophy, some of which were antisemitic and some of which were not. Nonetheless, some works, such as *The Protocols of the Elders of Zion*, depicted not only Zionists but Jews in general as pursuing not simply a Jewish state, but rather global power and domination via illegitimate and often criminal means. While antisemitism and anti-Zionism are not inherently related, there can indeed be connections and crossover between the two. This section will examine the historical development of political antisemitism in Germany and lead to an in-depth description of the current situation and problem.

As mentioned, *The Protocols of the Elders of Zion* in many ways originated modern political antisemitism and has indeed been a constant in the perpetuation of such beliefs. While *The Protocols* do invoke aspects of religious and economic antisemitism as well, the areas focusing on political power tend to be the most detailed sections and are what made *The Protocols* different from the sort of antisemitic propaganda published prior to the twentieth century. *The Protocols* were first published in Russia in 1903 as a fraudulent text purportedly chronicling the minutes of meetings between Zionist/Jewish leaders and detailed plans for a takeover of global political power.

The Protocols depicted the establishment of a "Jewish super-state" as a goal that would ultimately subvert and enslave all other peoples. However, *The Protocols* did not depict the establishment of a Jewish state as a legitimate political undertaking but rather a secretive conspiracy engineered for the ultimate goal of global domination and the submission of non-Jews. Protocol 7 stated, "The principal factor of success in the political is the secrecy of its undertakings" (Marsden, 2014: 26). Furthermore, *The Protocols* described the concept of a Jewish state as a sort of nightmare scenario leading to terror and death (Marsden, 2014: 12). The text also invoked a number of characteristic stereotypes of Jews regarding greed, cunning, and thievery—but broadened these stereotypes traditionally thought of in an economic sense and expanded them into the political realm. Whereas economic antisemitism tended to depict Jews as seeking illegitimate financial gain at the expense of others, political antisemitism, and *The Protocols* in particular, depicted Jews as seeking illegitimate political gain in the form of a "Jewish super-state" at the expense of others.

The Protocols were first published in German in 1920 and received immediate popularity, in part due to influential figures such as the Hohenzollern family, defraying publication costs and actively distributing copies throughout the country (Pipes, 1997: 95). *The Protocols* soon became an influential text during the Nazi rise to power and became widely studied in German schools (Segel and Levy, 1996: 42). *The Protocols* were especially effective in Germany, as they served the purpose of scapegoating Jewish conspiracies as the root cause of Germany's problems in the aftermath of World War I. As Nora Levin writes, "[*The Protocols*] were used to explain all of the disasters that had befallen the country: the defeat in the war, the hunger, the destructive inflation" (Levin, 1968: 19). Hitler even wrote of *The Protocols* in his *Mein Kampf* manifesto: "The important thing is that with positively terrifying certainty they reveal the nature and activity of the Jewish people and expose their inner contexts as well as their ultimate final aims" (Hitler, trans. 1998: 307–308). Joseph Goebbels similarly wrote that "the Zionist Protocols are as up to date today as they were the day they were first published" (Pipes, 1997: 95).

As with other forms of antisemitism, political antisemitism has persisted since the end of World War II; however, this particular form became increasingly complex, and perhaps in some ways has intensified, since the establishment of the State of Israel in 1948. One such way that political antisemitism has manifested itself in the post–World War II era has been through Holocaust denial. One argument common in Holocaust denial circles is that the Holocaust was either a hoax or at least greatly exaggerated by Jews in order to gain leverage in convincing Western powers to enable the establishment of a Jewish state—a goal outlined in *The Protocols* (Herf, 2013; Wistrich, 2012). In 1954, 13 percent of West Germans responded that they believed much of the Holocaust was exaggerated (Bergmann and Erb, 1997: 235). Holocaust denial theories received greater academic backing in the 1970s with the emergence of certain "revisionist" historians, such as Paul Rassinier and David Irving, who each questioned the statistics of those killed and Nazi culpability. Remarkably, data on Holocaust denial in Germany has remained consistent in the post–World War II era. In 1991, survey data demonstrated that 13 percent of Germans either agreed or somewhat agreed that Jews were at least partly to blame for their own persecution—the same percentage as in 1954 (Wetzel, 1997: 161).

Another manifestation of antisemitic attitudes is the questioning of Jews' loyalty to their home country. A common accusation is that Jews as a group are difficult, if not impossible, to assimilate due to "divided loyalties" between their fellow Jews and their attachment to their home country. For this reason, some have labeled Jews a "nation within a state" or a "state within a state" (Katz, 1969). With the establishment of Israel, this question of divided loyalties has stretched from not only loyalties to fellow Jews but also to Israel. A 1974 survey of West Germans asked whether or not respondents agreed or disagreed with the following statement: "Jews feel tied mainly to Israel. They are only marginally interested in the affairs of the country in which they live." Of those surveyed, 55 percent expressed either strong or mild agreement, while 30 percent expressed strong or mild disagreement, and 15 percent had no opinion (Bergmann and Erb, 1997: 145).

The same survey also asked respondents, "Would you consider a Jew born and raised in Germany more a German or more a Jew?" While 65 percent answered "more a German," 20 percent answered "more a Jew," and 15 percent were undecided. A 1982 survey posed a slightly different question: "Suppose there was a football game between Germany and Israel, and the spectators included German Jews. Whom do you think they would cross their fingers for, who would they root for?"

In response, 47 percent of the respondents believed the German Jews would root for Germany, 40 percent for Israel, and 13 percent were undecided (Bergmann and Erb, 1997: 130–131). While not necessarily overtly antisemitic behavior, the survey data do suggest a certain historical distrust among many Germans regarding Jews' loyalty to their home country and perhaps also a certain social distance between Germans and Jews. These suspicions among some Germans may lead some to "refuse to recognize German Jews as Germans, to deny them nationality" (Bergmann and Erb, 1997: 130). While this may in some cases be a subtler, nonviolent form of antisemitism, it can often be considered a hostile attitude toward Jews, thus meeting the operational definition established as part of this analysis.

3

Antisemitism in Poland

WHILE FOLLOWING THE STRUCTURE OF THE PREVIOUS CHAPTER, IN THIS chapter I not only examine the historical development and modern manifestations of antisemitism in Poland, but also identify certain differences with the German case.

Religious Antisemitism in Poland

The earliest mentions of Jews in Polish history date back to the tenth century, and their arrival was in large part a reaction to the persecution and antisemitism rampant across Europe at the time. Poland in many ways served as a refuge for European Jews, especially during the First Crusade in the late eleventh century. Whereas other parts of Europe had made Jews the subject of massacres, persecution, and banishment, Poland and its leaders had gained a reputation for tolerance and Jewish integration (Friedman, 2012: 9). However, it was not only Judaism that arrived in Poland at this time but also Christianity. Throughout its history, Poland had struggled with trying to ward off German expansion to the east, and one element of doing so was the first Polish King, Mieszko I, converting to Christianity in 966 in order to avoid armed conflict with the Saxons, who justified eastward expansion for the missionary purposes of converting pagan Poles (Cooper, 2000: 10). Therefore, it can be said that Judaism and Christianity arrived in Poland at nearly the same time, and their arrival was largely due to the religious persecution and missionary objectives of Poland's European neighbors.

Jews were generally welcomed into Polish territory in the centuries that followed in part due to a Polish adherence to the political value of tolerance, but also because of the desire of Polish leaders to harness the knowledge and expertise that many European Jews brought with them. This was especially the case under Bolesław III, who ruled Poland from 1102 to 1138 and actively sought out European Jews and their expertise in order to develop the Polish economy. Many Polish municipalities also incorporated what was known as the Magdeburg Law, which was a charter that allowed Jews, along with others, to live under certain legal protections and allowed Jews a prominent role in the local economy (Abramson, 2013). Such conditions made Poland an attractive destination for many Jews fleeing oppression, and this trend continued into the following centuries.

The tolerant environment that attracted many Jews to Poland was eventually affected by various influences, including the Roman Catholic Church and neighboring German states, which sought to roll back some of the tolerant policies that Poland had earlier adopted. The church's Councils of Wrocław (1267), Buda (1279), and Łęczyca (1285) put pressure on Polish leaders to implement restrictions on Jews by segregating them from the Christian population, ordering them to wear special emblems noting their religion, banning them from holding public office, and restricting the number of synagogues built (Dubnow, 2001: 44).

Such restrictions on Jews were not, however, universally enforced. A number of prominent Polish leaders continued to act as protectors of Jews from persecution despite directives from the church. For example, Duke Bolesław the Pious, the prince of Greater Poland, issued a General Charter of Jewish Liberties (known as the Statute of Kalisz) in 1264, which guaranteed Jews basic freedoms with regard to trade, travel, and worship, as well as outlined specific penalties for those who would physically or otherwise harm Polish Jews. The Statute of Kalisz was significant, in that it also led to the adoption of similar laws by leaders across Polish territory in the following decades (Dubnow, 2001: 45). So, while the Catholic Church did issue a number of decrees pushing for greater persecution of Polish Jewry, numerous Polish leaders, for various reasons, disobeyed these decrees and continued to maintain a relatively tolerant atmosphere for Jews compared to other parts of Europe.

Polish Jews were, nonetheless, targets of violent attacks due to religious motives such as blood libel, although to a lesser extent than in Germany. The first blood libel case recorded in Poland was in 1348, and this was followed soon after by the first pogrom in Poznań in 1367. Many Jews were also subjected to persecution around this time due to being scapegoated for the spread of the Black Death (Dubnow, 2001: 52). Such attacks were, however, discouraged and indeed punished by Polish leaders, namely King Casimir III the Great, who ruled from 1333 to 1370. So, while religious antisemitism was indeed present in Poland during the early Middle Ages, as it was elsewhere across Europe, the scale of violence was lessened, in part due to the policies of Polish leaders at the time. Tensions between the Catholic Church and various Polish rulers continued throughout the Middle Ages, and although there were occasional flare-ups of religious antisemitism and some localities were harsher to Jews than others, the Polish political value of tolerance largely prevented widespread, systematic persecution.

Although Polish leadership remained generally committed to protecting the state's Jewish community, flare-ups of antisemitic behavior remained evident during certain periods—and for the most part were motivated by religion. The fifteenth century in particular was marked by increases in Jewish persecution due to several factors, including dogmatic clergy pushing for less tolerance of Jews, the proliferation of blood libel accusations, and the continued scapegoating of Jews for spreading the Black Death (Dubnow, 2001: 22–24). In 1495, Jews were even ordered out of Krakow and were forced to resettle in the designated Jewish district of Kazimierz. Jews, for a period in the late fifteenth century, were also banished from Lithuania for a time. Near the end of the fifteenth century and early sixteenth, however, Polish leaders began to gravitate toward a policy of tolerance once again and removed many of the restrictions on Jewish life that had been implemented during the late fourteenth and early fifteenth centuries.

Throughout the seventeenth and eighteenth centuries, the Polish-Lithuanian Commonwealth was heavily impacted by violence due to the Cossack uprisings, as well as invasions by the Swedish, Russian, and Ottoman Empires. Throughout these conflicts, Poles and Jews were both heavily affected and incurred death tolls in the hundreds of thousands (Schultz, 1982: 268). Poland's Jewish community suffered a great deal, particularly during the Cossack uprisings, in large part due to the perception that Jews were allied with the Polish nobility (Hundert, 2004: 51). However, Polish rulers did remain generally supportive of Poland's Jewish community throughout the existence of the commonwealth, and Jews did not face the same sort of isolation as in other parts of Europe. In other words, Jews were often targeted by those opposing the Polish-Lithuanian state, rather than by the state itself.

Gershon Hundert describes the integration of Jews in the common-wealth by writing, "reports of romances, of drinking together in taverns, and of intellectual conversations [between Polish Catholics and Jews] were quite abundant" (Hundert, 2004: 51–52). However, the situation would later change due to the commonwealth's dissolution and the par-titioning of Poland by Prussia, Austria-Hungary, and Russia.

Following the Third Partition of Poland in 1795, the position of Jews in each partitioned territory differed. As Poland struggled to main-tain its independence in the late eighteenth century, many historians note that most Jews were not indifferent and indeed fought alongside Polish leadership against external invasions, and that this led to a cer-tain fraternity between many Poles and Jews (Orlicki, 1983: 21). How-ever, Poland was eventually conquered by its neighbors and divided into three territories controlled by Prussia, Austria-Hungary, and Russia. The Prussian area was home to only a negligible population of Jews, but the Jews in the Prussian section were largely given equal rights. In the Aus-tro-Hungarian section, Jews were prohibited from using the Yiddish or Hebrew languages in all public or legal institutions, but other than these restrictions were also provided equal rights. In the Russian section, Jews faced far greater restrictions on the practice of their religion and were pressured to integrate and, in many cases, convert to Christianity (Cooper, 2000: 24–25). Jews were restricted to living only within an area known as the Pale of Settlement, and the Russian czars put great emphasis on attempting to assimilate the Jewish population of their newly acquired territory. The czars took such actions as prohibiting Hebrew or Yiddish curricula in schools, expelling Jews from many vil-lages, and conscripting Jewish children as young as twelve years old into the military. Between 1827 and 1857, over 30,000 Jewish children were placed in military schools, in which they were pressured to con-vert to Christianity (Petrovsky-Shtern, 2009). There were indeed other manifestations of antisemitism from the late eighteenth through early twentieth century; however, the primary means through which religious antisemitism specifically arose were through these restrictions on reli-gious practice, resettlement, and pressured conversion.

With the collapse of the German, Austro-Hungarian, and Russian Empires at the end of World War I, Poland was able to establish an independent state once again in 1918. Jews played a major role in the Polish liberation movement, and many actively served under the direc-tion of Józef Piłsudski, the movement's leader. The establishment of the newly independent Poland did, however, pose a major challenge to the resident Jewish community as Catholicism became more closely linked to Polish national identity. As western Europe became increasingly secular after the Age of Enlightenment, Polish society tended to trend in the opposite direction, with Catholicism becoming increasingly linked to Polish patriotism (Smolar, 1987: 32). The Jewish historian Jacob Shatzky wrote: "Under the political conditions of the time, assimilation did not mean merely embracing Polish culture. The Roman Catholic Church played too important a role in the preservation of Polish culture to make it possible to separate Catholicism from Polonism" (Lichten, 1986: 112). Consequently, many Jews, in order to assimilate, began to adopt the majority faith of Catholicism. As Leo Cooper writes, "In the nineteenth and early twentieth centuries conversion meant a final step toward unity with the Polish people" (Cooper, 2000: 37). Many Poles, however, viewed Jewish assimilation as an infiltration of Polish culture by a group that held alien and hostile values. This led to an increased emphasis on the "Jewish Question" among the Polish intelligentsia. The prevailing belief among the conservative, clergy-dominated faction advocated that Jews "renounce their religion and their national peculiarity in favor of complete assimilation or that they should leave Poland" (Cooper, 2000: 38). Therefore, in the aftermath of World War I and the establishment of the newly independent Poland, the Polish political value of religious tolerance began to erode as Jewishness became increasingly disassociated from and unwelcomed as part of Polish national identity.

Poland during the interwar period experienced severe conflict between those who sought to uphold the political value of tolerance and pluralism and those who sought to establish a Catholic state of the Polish nation. As part of the Paris Peace Conference, a Minority Rights clause was applied to Poland with special mention of Jewish minorities, who accounted for nearly 10 percent of the country's total population (Tomicki, 1982: 310). Piłsudski, commonly viewed as the liberator of Poland and eventual leader after a 1926 coup, tended to adhere to the value of tolerance and acted as a protector of the Jewish community. However, Piłsudski was in conflict with the National Democrats, who held that only those of the Polish race and Christian beliefs qualified for citizenship (Black, 1987: 15). The National Democrats had substantial support among university students, the Polish intelligentsia, as well as many among the clergy. In fact, Polish bishops issued a pastoral letter on December 5, 1927, calling on all Catholics to support the antisemitic National Democrats in upcoming elections (Cooper, 2000: 49). A core belief of the National Democrats was that a Pole was meant to be a Christian, and a Jew was an alien element distinct from a Pole.

After Piłsudski's death in 1935, the situation for Poland's Jewish community drastically worsened as the National Democrats and their supporters seized the opportunity to push for the establishment of a Catholic state and sought to provide an answer to the Jewish Question. Anti-Jewish student campaigns, largely supported by the Catholic Church, organized a pilgrimage to the town of Częstochowa in 1936 that attracted 60,000 students, or 60 percent of all Polish university students. At the demonstration, the students vowed "to build a Catholic state of the Polish nation" and declared that "we will not rest until the last Jew, alive or dead, has left Polish soil" (Cooper, 2000: 59). Catholic publications also emphasized the religious aspects of the Jewish Question by publishing numerous articles on the immorality of the Talmud and the destructive nature of Jewish ethics and culture (Cooper, 2000: 62). Many Polish Catholics viewed Jews as the primary obstacle to their goal of an official Catholic state of Poland. Consequently, the demonization of the Jewish religion, which for centuries had been largely tolerated in Polish society, became a powerful and widespread tool in controlling crowds and igniting passions.

By the time of the Nazi invasion of Poland in 1939, significant cleavages existed between segments of Poland's Catholic and Jewish populations; however, not all Poles were uniform in their relations with Jews. The Nazi German invocations of religious antisemitism, commonly based on the writings of Martin Luther, did not have equal resonance in Poland due to the differing religious traditions in each country. Nonetheless, many Jews had already been alienated by certain Catholic nationalist segments of Polish society. Although the goal of a Catholic Polish state diminished with the Nazi occupation, the Nazis were able to exploit tensions between Poles and Jews. Despite unsuccessful attempts to enlist official Polish collaboration, some Poles were cooperative in Nazi German plans for the deportation of Jews and the implementation of the Final Solution. Groups such as the Blue Police actively assisted the Nazis in capturing, deporting, and even executing Jews (Ringelblum, 1985: 309–310).

Nonetheless, elements of the Polish resistance differed in the treatment of Jews; while some reports claim that Polish resistance movements were responsible for executing Jews, other groups, such as Żegota, were known to have made rescuing Jews a primary mission. Many of those who viewed Jews as a hindrance, or even enemy, of the Polish state during the interwar period continued to do so during the Nazi occupation (Cooper, 2000: 144–147). Meanwhile, groups such as Żegota would often invoke Catholicism as a means to protect Polish Jews. One of the cofounders of Żegota wrote that "anyone who remains silent is an accomplice; he who does not condemn condones" (Tomaszewski and Werbowski, 1994: 13). Other Żegota literature stated that one who does "not support our protest is not a Catholic" (Prekerowa, 1992: 162). So, while religion's role in Polish society often served as a point of tension between Catholics and Jews, others viewed religion as a call to aid the persecuted Jewish population.

The Holocaust decimated Poland's Jewish population, reducing the 1939 number of 3.6 million to only about 100,000 by 1945 (Yivo Institute for Jewish Research, 2023b). Nonetheless, anti-Jewish violence continued within Poland's borders due to a series of blood libel rumors through 1946 reminiscent of events centuries earlier. The Krakow pogrom commenced on August 11, 1945, following accusations that a Jewish woman attempted to kidnap a Polish child and the alleged discovery of corpses of Christian children in a local synagogue. This led to riots in the city, in which at least one Jew was killed, and a synagogue was set aflame (Cichopek, 2003: 224). This event was followed by blood libel accusations and violence in about a dozen Polish towns—the most fraught and impactful of which occurred in the town of Kielce (Piotrowski, 1997: 136). The brutality of the Kielce pogrom led many of the remaining Polish Jews to emigrate and begin a new life abroad. By spring 1947, tens of thousands of Poland's remaining Jews had fled, leading to a virtual absence of the country's Jewish community that had existed for nearly a millennium (Bernhard and Szlajfer, 2004).

In the decades during communist rule in Poland, the state was known to exploit antisemitism for various political purposes, but religious antisemitism typically gave way to other manifestations. There is no reliable data available that traced antisemitic trends in communist Poland and also few examples of religious antisemitism motivating incidents of violence, in part due to the relative lack of Jews in the country during this time and also a general de-emphasis of religion during communist rule. However, data taken since the fall of communism has shown that religious antisemitism, in particular allegations of deicide, tend to have greater resonance in Poland than anywhere in western Europe. A 2005 survey conducted by the Anti-Defamation League showed that Poland had nearly twice as many respondents (39 percent) answer "yes" to the statement "Jews are responsible for the death of Christ" than the next highest country Denmark (22 percent) (Anti-Defamation League, 2005). The fact that religious antisemitism is higher in Poland than most countries seems to correlate with the fact that Poland also remains one of the most religious countries in

Europe: 87.5 percent of Poles claim Catholicism as their religion, with 43 percent attending church services at least once per week and 76 percent attending several times per year (Statistics Poland, 2019; Public Opinion Research Center, 2021). While there have not been any significant incidents of blood libel since the Kielce pogrom in 1946, the fact that deicide remains a major source of antisemitism in Poland demonstrates that the religious manifestation of the problem continues to remain an issue, and substantially more so than in countries with lower levels of religiosity.

Economic Antisemitism in Poland

Ever since their arrival in Poland a millennium ago, Jews have played an integral role in the development of the Polish economy. In fact, historians frequently cite the productivity and expertise of the Jewish community as a primary reason for Poland's welcoming attitude toward Jews and longstanding emphasis on religious tolerance (Cooper, 2000: 10). Polish kings were known to have implemented certain policies to attract western European Jews to help develop the primitive Polish economy in the thirteenth century—the Statute of Kalisz being one example of such a policy (Abramsky, Jachimczyk, and Polonsky, 1986: 3). At a time of near universal illiteracy, European Jews were able to bring certain knowledge and economic expertise to Poland, and in return they received the promise of a tolerant society in which to live. Many of the Jews who settled in Poland came from Germany and had an expertise in finance due to the reasons described in Chapter 2. Consequently, historical records indicate that Jews were granted the minting of Polish coins as early as the twelfth century. And as towns began to rise in the thirteenth and fourteenth centuries, Jews were often responsible for helping obtain the capital and financial resources necessary to develop industries, primarily agriculture, for the nobility (Cooper, 2000: 11–12). These factors led to Jews commonly assuming prominent roles in the Polish economy, but this reality has also led to certain grievances and resentment among some known as economic antisemitism.

The relative success of Jews in Poland's economy resulted in resentments focusing on the competition that Jews posed to Christian merchants. Pamphlets in the sixteenth and seventeenth centuries often combined religious accusations against Jews and a focus on economic competition. These sorts of arguments tended to depict mere Jewish participation in commerce as a crime. Common arguments were that Jews "take the trade away from the city [and the Christian merchants]" and "corrupt judges with gifts and the lords with bowing" (Mahler, 1942: 116; Hundert, 1986: 49). Such arguments not only depicted Jews as a threat to the economic well-being of Christians, but also undermined the legitimacy and ethics of Jewish involvement in commerce.

As Poland was occupied and partitioned by its neighbors in the late eighteenth century, Jews provided a convenient scapegoat for the economic misery experienced across Polish territory. Even though many Jews fought alongside Polish nationalists to maintain the sovereignty of the Polish state, antisemitic propaganda began circulating in the late eighteenth century demanding the expulsion of Jews from the cities and that they be resettled as peasants or laborers on public works projects. These pamphlets described Jewish economic influence as "the plague," a "contagion," and "putridness." A common argument in such literature was that Jews were "taking away the bread from Christians" and thus needed to be subjugated to a lower rung of the economic ladder (Mahler, 1942: 126). These types of arguments asserted that the Polish economy's reliance on Jews in various sectors was an inherent weakness that enabled the fall of the sovereign Polish state. This became a popular theme and expression of economic antisemitism among nationalist movements.

Economic antisemitism continued into the twentieth century, in large part due to the influence of the National-Democratic Party and its exploitation of antisemitic feelings. Even prior to World War I and the establishment of a newly sovereign Poland, the National Democrats began organizing economic boycotts against Jews in 1909. Common slogans of the group were "Do not buy from the Jews!" and "stick to your own kind" (Cooper, 2000: 32). However, the stereotype that Jews consisted entirely of rich people, as was common in western Europe, tended to have less resonance in Poland, due to the dire poverty that many Jews in small towns and the Jewish districts of major cities experienced. Still, Polish antisemitic groups depicted the lower-class living conditions of many Jews as a threat to the future of Polish society. Polish historian Teodor Jeske-Choiński explained the poverty of Polish Jews as follows: "Amidst the cold and frost the Jew lives a whole day on a piece of herring, on a crumb of bread watered down with brandy and greased with a head of onion or garlic. A Polish dog would die with such a diet, yet the Jew feels fine and multiplies like sand on the seashore" (1913: 90). This sort of depiction painted Jews as a sort of pest that "multiplies" despite their living conditions or economic well-being. In other words, economic antisemitism could be aimed at Jews of varying economic classes—the stereotype of the greedy, wealthy Jew on one hand and the "multiplying," impoverished Jew on the other—with both constituting threats to Polish society.

Even before the Second Polish Republic was established in 1918, the National Democrats had in their platform plans to "de-Judaize" the Polish economy, but in the 1920s the emphasis on such a program increased drastically as the newly independent Poland engaged in active conflict with the Russian Bolsheviks. As conflict between Poland and Soviet Russia broke into a full-scale war in 1920, Polish Jews overwhelmingly supported the Polish war effort with many serving in the military on the front lines. Nonetheless, even as the Soviet Army withdrew, many Poles continued to accuse Jews of collaboration with the Bolsheviks. Such accusations were part of widespread propaganda that proclaimed Bolshevism was a creation of the Jews. Common antisemitic propaganda at the time depicted Red Army soldiers carrying white and blue flags with the Star of David (Cooper, 2000: 45). Such propaganda was accompanied by pogroms in numerous cities, and military tribunals were set up to prosecute alleged Jewish "spies," many of whom were executed (Cooper, 2000: 45). Given the historical tensions between Poland and Russia, tying the Jewish community in Poland with the Bolshevik ideology acted as a means to create an enemy by alleged association. The accusation that Jews are a disloyal and untrustworthy group due to certain minority characteristics is a common theme in economically antisemitic rhetoric and ideology, and forging connections between Polish Jews and Bolshevism only served to exacerbate such attitudes.

Antisemitic sentiment in Poland was also fueled in the 1920s and 1930s by the onset of the Great Depression. Polish Jews provided a convenient scapegoat for the widespread unemployment and dire economic circumstances across the country. The same themes of Jews being depicted as competitors and exploiters of other Poles were common, even though the living conditions and income levels of Polish Jews were on average lower than for most other Polish industrial workers (Gutman, Mendelsohn, and Shmeruk, 1989: 102). As jobs became increasingly scarce for all workers in Poland, the situation was even worse for Jews due to increasing employment discrimination. While Jews accounted for 10 percent of Poland's population in 1923, only 2.23 percent of government employees were Jewish, and that number declined to only 1 percent by 1930. Furthermore, Jews accounted for 30 percent of Poland's urban population, but only 2 to 3 percent of municipal employees (Ben-Sasson, 1976: 955–956). There were even reports of Jews being denied employment opportunities at Jewish-owned businesses due to the objections and unwillingness of some Christian workers to work with Jews. There were also numerous boycotts of Jewish shops and signs placed on certain storefronts to denote the religion of the owner (Cooper, 2000: 53). The dire economic circumstances of the Great Depression allowed a number of historical manifestations of economic antisemitism to arise once again and, in many cases, intensify. At a time when the newly established Polish state was struggling with questions regarding the role of religion in the state's identity, the dire economic circumstances of the depression led to both the religious and economic manifestations of antisemitism to complement one another and grow.

Knowing that antisemitic sentiment had grown in Poland during the interwar period, the Nazis exploited tensions between Poles and Jews in order to carry out their goals in implementing the Final Solution. A primary area upon which the Nazis focused was tension over economic competition between Poles and Jews. Soon after the Nazis had overtaken Warsaw, the German NSV (National-Sozialistische Volkswohlfahrt) organized centers for the free distribution of bread. These bread lines were created not only for propaganda purposes, but also to stoke feelings of economic antisemitism. In order to shorten the queues, Poles were incentivized to identify the Jews among them and have the Jews removed from the queue (Ringelblum, 1985: 255). Economic incentives were also a common tactic used by the Nazis to coerce Poles into providing information about their Jewish neighbors. Severe penalties, including death, were commonly applied to those hiding Jews, but monetary and other awards, including the belongings of captured Jews, were promised as bounties. This was a common tactic, particularly in rural areas, where virtually all residents knew one another (Ringelblum, 1985: 313). Many Polish peasants also benefited from Nazi policies that canceled debts owed to Jewish creditors and that eliminated certain taxes (Cooper, 2000: 91).

Consequently, some historians cite economic antisemitism as a primary reason why many Poles did not provide greater resistance to the Nazi atrocities committed against Polish Jews. As Richard Lukas wrote:

> Despite German persecution of the Polish people, a small minority of Poles openly approved of German policies toward Jews, and some actively aided the Nazis in their task. Other Poles showed no outward pleasure at the removal of Jews from Polish offices, professions, and businesses but were not opposed to the economic expropriation involved. These people had antisemitic views which were

economic, not racial, in character; it reflected an economic antisemitic attitude. (1986: 126)

Therefore, while many Poles did not actively seek, or even participate in, the atrocities committed against Polish Jewry by the Nazis,
some were accepting of the removal of Jews from economically significant positions—similar to the process to "de-Judaize" the economy
that had been an emphasis of the National Democrats since the early
twentieth century. So, in many ways, the exploitation of economic
antisemitism by the Nazis was not necessarily a new concept within
Polish society, but rather the Nazis worked to exploit enduring economic tensions between Poles and Jews, particularly as it relates to
economic competition.

Although nearly all of Poland's pre–World War II Jewish community was either killed in the Holocaust or had emigrated soon after the
war, economic antisemitism and Jewish persecution in general did not
cease under the postwar communist government. Following Stalin's
death and the consolidation of communist rule in Poland, there were
a number of workers' disturbances in the city of Poznań and a general
discontent among the Polish people regarding the failures of Stalinism
and the communist system. After assuming power in 1956, the government under Władysław Gomułka began to search for a scapegoat to
divert public attention away from domestic economic failures and
ineffective policy measures. The legacy of the preceding decades
made Jews an easy target, and thus an antisemitic campaign was
unleashed (Cooper, 2000: 206–207). The Gomułka government purged
Jews from top positions in the party, sensitive posts in the government, as well as from the army (Dawidowicz, 1983: 97). In 1950,
there were only about 45,000 Jews left in Poland, with more emigrating in subsequent years. Yet even though Poland had been nearly rid-
den of its pre–World War II Jewish population, antisemitism continued
to exist in an environment nearly absent of Jews (Cooper, 2000: 206).
Thus, it was not necessarily the presence of Jews that spurred the antisemitic sentiment under the communist regime, but rather a historical
legacy of antisemitism and conspiratorial beliefs about the role and
influence of Jews in society.

Antisemitic propaganda became characteristic of the communist
government's strategy, not only for the purpose of scapegoating a particular people for the regime's failures but also to seize property and
wages and exploit domestic economic competition in much the same
way as the Nazis and the National Democrats. Poland's communist

leaders, and especially the Gomułka government, enacted a campaign of psychological terror on Polish Jews in order to pressure emigration. All Jews in communist Poland were registered by the Ministry of Internal Affairs and were pressured to emigrate via anonymous letters, phone calls, threats, loss of employment, and vandalism. Consequently, many Jews committed suicide, families became separated, and those who did decide to emigrate were often left little choice but to sell their possessions to state-owned shops for excessively low prices. Many Poles benefited from the economic oppression of the Jewish population by obtaining the jobs and occupying the homes of fleeing Jews—similar to the circumstances during the Nazi occupation. Such conditions damaged the image of Poland abroad, so the government initiated counter-propaganda claiming that such persecution did not exist. In 1968, Polish diplomat Jan Druto claimed in Paris that "the majority of the tiny Jewish community was deeply attached to their country" (Cooper, 2000: 220–224). So, while the communist government attempted to portray a positive image abroad, its antisemitic agenda domestically went beyond mere scapegoating and into outright economic persecution reminiscent of the Nazi occupation.

Racial Antisemitism in Poland

Although racial antisemitism in Poland historically tended to lack the sort of pseudoscientific eugenics element of the German variety, ethnic nationalism was often a key motivation behind antisemitism in Poland throughout the twentieth century. Racial antisemitism is one of the more recent manifestations to arise in the Polish case, not having taken hold with great affect until the rise of the National Democrats and formation of the newly independent state in 1918. The establishment of the new Polish state reignited debate over what it meant to be Polish, and, further, what place minority populations had in such a state. As with many nationalist movements, culture played a central role in the debate of what constituted "Polishness." Despite the fact that Jews had historically been influential in Poland's intellectual and cultural circles, many viewed such influence as illegitimate and not sufficiently reflective of the typical Pole. Those Jews who sought to assimilate, even via conversion to Christianity, would often be dismissed as not true Poles. Therefore, in many cases antisemitism stretched beyond merely a prejudice of certain beliefs or values, and into the realm of prejudice against one's ethnic makeup or inherent "Jewishness."

In the nineteenth century, many Polish Jews sought to fully assimilate with the majority of Poles and thus spoke the Polish language, adopted the culture, and even converted to Christianity (Lichten, 1986: 112). However, not all Poles welcomed such a development. Many Poles became concerned about what they believed to be the "Jewification" of Polish culture—that Jews were intruding on Polish identity (Cooper, 2000: 37). These sorts of allegations parallel those in Germany by figures such as Richard Wagner, who had similar concerns in the German case. Although the sorts of pseudoscientific theories that were widespread in Germany did not achieve equal prominence in Poland, the Polish intelligentsia, and especially university students, became some of the most vehement propagators of racial antisemitism.

Amid concerns that Jews were "polluting" the Polish culture and entering higher education in excessive numbers, Poznań University implemented a discriminatory quota system in 1919 that limited the number of Jews who could attend university. This policy was followed by rallies at numerous other universities across the country where students demanded similar policies be implemented. In February 1928, students at Krakow University demanded complete segregation of Jews at the university, and following violent clashes at Warsaw University, the quota system expanded across the country. By 1931, the National Democrats and various student groups were no longer calling for quota systems, but for the total elimination of Jews from Polish universities (Cooper, 2000: 56–59). As the Nazis rose to power in neighboring Germany in the 1930s, universities in Poland became the one area of Polish society where Nazi racial propaganda most resonated. In spring 1937, amid pressure from student organizations, university rectors and deans introduced special seating for Jewish students nicknamed "ghetto benches" that fomented an atmosphere of constant harassment. By 1938, students of Jewish origin (not only Jewish faith) were barred from joining student organizations. At this time, students also began demanding that anti-Jewish legislation similar to the Nuremberg Laws be enacted in Poland (Rudnicki, 1987: 264). The sort of ethnic nationalism on the campuses of many Polish universities in the early twentieth century mirrored many of the developments in Germany at the time and made these campuses particularly fertile grounds for the propagation of racial antisemitism. Universities became one of the first institutions in Poland where Jews became discriminated against not only for their faith and beliefs, but also for their racial and ethnic makeup.

A primary reason behind the growing popularity of ethnic nationalism in early twentieth century Poland was a certain level of distrust among many Poles for Jews regardless of any efforts they made toward assimilation. This dynamic put Polish Jews in a precarious position: either be accused of separateness on the one hand or of intrusion into Polish culture on the other (Cooper, 2000: 52). This sort of no-win situation is characteristic of racial antisemitism—whereas one can change one's beliefs, one cannot change one's ethnicity—thus, racial antisemitism allows for no remedy. These factors make violence particularly likely in cases where racial antisemitism manifests. Even prior to the Nazi occupation of Poland, there were a series of pogroms across the country from 1934 to 1939 where 500 Jews were murdered (30 of whom were university students) and about 5,000 were wounded (Cooper, 2000: 67). In some instances, Jews did resist the violence perpetrated against them, but these actions were often futile, as any Christian casualties were often treated as an act for which Jews would be held collectively responsible (Gutman, Mendelsohn, and Shmeruk, 1989: 129).

The ethnic nationalism within interwar Poland in some ways paralleled the racially antisemitic propaganda of Nazi Germany. In fact, one Polish parliamentarian in 1936 proposed a plan that would deprive Jews of civil rights, confiscate assets, and incarcerate about 600,000 Jews in concentration camps (Cooper, 2000: 72). This plan was intended to not only persecute domestic Jews, but also create conditions pressuring the rest to emigrate. Although these measures were merely a proposal, there was indeed traction for such ideas within ethnic nationalist segments of the Polish population.

While Nazi racial ideology did consider ethnic Poles to be on a lower stratum of the Aryan race, Poles were nonetheless considered Aryan, and thus there remained a clear divide between Poles and Jews during the Nazi occupation. The Nazis did indeed commit massacres targeting the leading strata of Polish society, but such actions were largely not taken against unskilled workers, peasants, and others who could essentially be forced to work under Nazi leadership (Gross, 1979: 76). Jews, on the other hand, were targeted for extermination, regardless of occupation or skill. Thus, the Nazi targeting of Poles was intended to ensure submissiveness and obedience, whereas Nazi targeting of Jews was intended to result in absolute extermination.

The living conditions within Nazi-occupied Poland were intended to foment an atmosphere in which animosity between Poles and Jews was exploited. In cities, Jews were confined to the Jewish ghettos, while Poles lived on the Aryan side. Jews on the Aryan side lived in an extremely dangerous situation, as the consequences of being caught were universally severe. The Nazis applied a carrot and stick method to coerce Poles into turning over fugitive or hidden Jews, and the sheer terror and psychological stress of avoiding recognition led many Jews to return to the ghettos (Ringelblum, 1985: 291). Necessities as simple as seeing a doctor when ill were particularly dangerous, as there were numerous cases of doctors reporting Jewish patients to authorities (Ringelblum, 1985: 300). Such an atmosphere conditioned many Poles to believe, or at least live by, the Nazi ideology that viewed Jews as inherently lesser and devalued human beings.

Following the end of World War II and the Holocaust, the sort of racial antisemitism that had been so prominent during the Nazi occupation lessened greatly, but did nonetheless leave a certain legacy, as in the German case. Racial antisemitism did not play a major role in the antisemitic propaganda under communist rule, although some survey data and rhetoric from antisemitic groups have shown that racial antisemitism continued to exist. Data on antisemitism in communist Poland is scarce, but a 1988 survey showed that 23 percent of Poles would not accept a blood transfusion from a Jew and 40 percent would advise a friend against marrying a Jew. By 1998, however, these numbers dropped to 15 percent and 33 percent respectively (Sulek, 2012: 431). There also remains a fascination or even admiration among some antisemitic Poles for the Nazi agenda toward Jews, as evidenced by certain incidents attacking Jewish interests. In September 1990, a monument erected at the *Umschlagplatz* in Warsaw, where 350,000 Jews were sent to concentration camps, was defaced by graffiti with the words "a good Jew is a dead Jew." Around the same time in Warsaw, youth demonstrators burned the effigy of Prime Minister Józef Oleksy decorated with a Star of David and shouted that Jews ought to once again be sent to the gas chambers (Cooper, 2000: 226). These sorts of incidents continue to be a symptom of racial antisemitism and the belief that Jews as an ethnicity or race deserve to be discriminated against or attacked. While racial antisemitism may not be the predominant form in the Polish case, it is historically one of the most violent manifestations and therefore remains an important problem where it exists regardless of its prominence.

Political Antisemitism in Poland

Political antisemitism is the belief that Jews are in constant pursuit of global political power for mischievous purposes and is often complemented by conspiracy theories and scapegoating. As in the German case, this strain of antisemitism rose to prominence in Poland during the twentieth century and has been heavily influenced by reactions to Zionism. Polish ethnic nationalism of the early twentieth century sought to create a homogenous Catholic state in which Jews were unwelcome. In order to attract followers, the National Democrats and other ethnic nationalists exploited suspicions about Poland's Jewish community and their loyalty to the country. As nationalist discrimination against Jews increased in the 1920s and 1930s, a growing number of Jews joined the Zionist movement, which only exacerbated nationalist suspicions and led some to believe that Jews were more loyal to Zionism than Poland (Cooper, 2000: 72). This dynamic was influential in decreasing social trust between Poles and Jews and gave rise to conspiracy theories about the ultimate aims of Polish Jews.

Beginning in the 1930s, the idea of forced, or at least strongly pressured, emigration gained traction among Polish antisemitic groups and individuals. At times, these groups and individuals have advocated distorted versions of Zionism to justify their motives and accomplish their goals. In 1936, the Polish government at the annual meeting of the League of Nations even proposed a scheme demanding the allocation of colonies where Polish Jews could be resettled. Only one month later, Józef Beck, Poland's minister of foreign affairs, made an official request to international banks to help finance a mass emigration of Polish Jews (Cooper, 2000: 72). These were proposed answers to the Jewish Question in interwar Poland. However, whereas Zionism typically implies voluntary Jewish resettlement to a designated homeland, many of the proposals at this time called for a forcible resettlement.

The calls for forced Jewish emigration were not limited to one decade and indeed carried on throughout twentieth-century Poland, despite the various periods of foreign occupation. One of the most prominent examples of political antisemitism and its influence is demonstrated by the case of Polish politician Bolesław Piasecki. Piasecki was the leader of the ultranationalist National Radical Camp-Falanga party, founded in 1935, and called for the "systematic and radical elimination of Jews from Poland" (Cooper, 2000: 208). Piasecki's goal was to facilitate an anti-Jewish atmosphere in Poland that would force a mass exodus of Polish Jews and "free" Poland from the perceived Jewish influence in government and society (Gutman, Mendelsohn, and Shmeruk, 1989: 9). Piasecki and his movement, however, were not constrained to the 1930s. Although the National Radical Camp-Falanga party disappeared during the Nazi occupation, Poland's postwar communist government adopted many of the same themes in anti-Jewish propaganda. In 1947, Piasecki founded the PAX Association that carried on a similar ideology, albeit with a more procommunist stance. Piasecki was even appointed a member of the Council of State of the Polish People's Republic—the supreme state authority—and became an important figure in stirring up the antisemitic propaganda of the communist regime (Cooper, 2000: 208). Piasecki is only one example but is nonetheless a personification of the sort of political anti-semitism that manifested in Poland in the early twentieth century and has survived despite periods of foreign occupation.

As discussed in the preceding sections, each manifestation of anti-semitism had a presence around the time of the Holocaust and its imme-diate aftermath, but political antisemitism in particular increased fol-lowing the establishment of the State of Israel. This was especially true in 1967 in the aftermath of the Six-Day War. Many Poles celebrated the decisive Israeli victory, not necessarily out of a love for Jews or Israel itself, but rather the perceived setback suffered by the communists and their allies. Some Poles were even happy that what they considered "our Jews"—those who used to reside in Poland—were responsible for the communist setback (Kunicki, 2012: 153–155; Cooper, 2000: 209). This reaction was met with discontent from the communist regime, which responded by initiating a mass campaign of antisemitic propaganda dis-guised as anti-Zionism.

In June 1967, the Gomułka government publicly criticized Jews as a potentially dangerous "fifth column," and as people having "two fatherlands" and a "double allegiance" who therefore could not be trusted (Cooper, 2000: 209). These accusations served as a pretext for the removal from the party and administrative posts of any member who was considered to be of Jewish origin. Although according to Polish law at the time individuals were not required to state their religion on iden-tity documents, the government nonetheless compiled a confidential list of those considered Jewish based on information supplied by other Poles (Banas, 1979: 90). The environment of antisemitic persecution created by the Gomułka government contributed to the mass exodus of many of the remaining Polish Jews—a situation that the government further exploited to serve its propaganda messaging. Those Jews who did decide to emigrate were often coerced into making statements and signing documents that depicted them as disloyal and even treasonous. Each Jewish applicant for emigration was forced to sign a document renouncing their Polish citizenship and asked to declare that they felt more affinity to Israel than Poland (even those not emigrating to Israel) (Dawidowicz, 1983: 110). These sorts of measures notably aligned with the themes propagated in texts such as *The Protocols of the Elders of Zion*, which continues to be distributed in antisemitic circles within Poland (Cooper, 2000: 211). In short, these measures sought to more closely connect anti-Zionism with antisemitism by depicting Jews as collectively disloyal to Poland and its national interests.

This emphasis on antisemitism by the communists served an additional purpose of the government, which was to keep nationalist sentiment subdued. Nationalist movements throughout central and eastern Europe were a potential threat to Soviet-directed communist governments, and one means of placating such movements was by identifying a common "enemy," which had for many nationalists historically been the Jewish community. As Leo Cooper writes, "Nationalism requires the existence of an enemy of the nation; antisemitism served that purpose" (2000: 219). The antisemitic campaign by the state was in part intended to take nationalist aggression toward the regime and redirect it toward Jews. However, such measures were not entirely successful, as many nationalist movements continued to hold antipathy toward the regime, but others such as the PAX Association led by Piasecki did align with the communist-led antisemitic campaign and supported the government's actions.

Unlike in the German case, Holocaust denial tends to be much less prevalent in Poland (European Parliamentary Research Service, 2020). The controversy, however, tends to lie in how the victims should be honored and who exactly the victims of the camps were. Controversy arose at Auschwitz in 1989 when Catholics erected a cross at the camp during a visit by Pope John Paul II. Those in support of the cross's placement argued that it was to honor the 100,000 Poles killed at the camp, while others see the cross as a means to discount the more than 1 million Jews killed there. By 1998, there were approximately 240 crosses placed at the site, and the resulting controversy created even greater tension between Poles and Jews over the question of who suffered more under the Nazi occupation (Zubrzycki, 2006). Casimir Svitin, the caretaker of the crosses, has expressed certain antisemitic rhetoric and conspiracy theories about Jews and has even stated that the crosses are an act of defiance against Jewish influence in Poland. Svitin has argued that "the Jews want to exploit us, they want to take power in Poland, but these Christian symbols prove that we will not submit to their blackmail" (Cooper, 2000: 233). Others have been even more forceful in denouncing sympathy for the Jewish Holocaust, such as Henryk Jankowski, a Gdańsk-area priest, who stated "the shield of David is intertwined with the swastika in the same way as is the sickle and the hammer" (Cooper, 2000: 230). So, while Holocaust denial tends to be less common in the Polish case, many view sympathy for the victims as a sort of zero-sum game where it is either Poles or Jews viewed as victims of the genocide but not both. Themes of political antisemitism also seep into this controversy with statements, such as those by Svitin, which claim that Jews attempt to exploit sympathies over the Holocaust as means to political power. This is a common argument among Polish nationalists who continue to view Jews as a threat to Polish national interests, despite the contemporary Jewish community in the country numbering only a few thousand.

Survey data demonstrate that indeed political antisemitism remains a prominent manifestation of antisemitism in Poland. In 1992, 38 percent of Poles surveyed answered that they "would absolutely not vote for a presidential candidate of Jewish descent." This number only declined to 33 percent by 2002 (Sulek, 2012: 431). In 1992, 18 percent of Poles surveyed agreed with the statement "Poles had experienced more bad from Jews than good," and this number actually rose to 27 percent by 2002 (Sulek, 2012: 431). A 1999 survey showed that a majority (56 percent) of Poles surveyed either responded "strongly agree" or "somewhat agree" with the statement "Now, as in the past, Jews exert too much influence on world events" (Sulek, 2012: 436). As can be seen, regardless of the number of Jews actually residing in Poland, a substantial segment of the population of modern Poland continued to believe that Jews exert excessive influence on the country's political affairs even after the fall of communism. While there is little to no survey data available from the time period of communist occupation in Poland, it is likely that the antisemitic propaganda of the previous regimes continues to have a legacy in the country in terms of perceptions and distrust toward the Jewish community.

The ability to "come to terms with the past" and confront the forms of hatred that have resulted in the deaths of millions remains a major challenge. Both Germany and Poland continue to struggle with addressing these fraught issues that have developed over centuries. Nonetheless, both countries have made efforts, however varied, to address these challenges in recent years. The following chapters of this analysis will explore some of these measures and seek to evaluate how antisemitic attitudes and actions have consequently been affected.

4

Germany Combats Antisemitism

As the preceding chapters explained, antisemitism has been a pervasive issue in Germany and Poland for centuries. Consequently, this issue has shaped many international perceptions about these countries and their people. This is certainly a negative perception that can undermine attempts at cooperation in many areas. As Germany and Poland emerged from the Cold War era, both countries sought to improve their international standing, and part of doing so required addressing the fraught aspects of each country's history, in particular antisemitism and the Holocaust.

In the early post–Cold War period, the newly reunified Germany faced numerous political, social, and economic challenges. Antisemitism, while commonly viewed as a social problem, can indeed affect a country's standing in other areas to the extent that perceptions of pervasive antisemitism among international actors undermines their cooperation and trust. Consequently, responding to accusations and the realities of antisemitism domestically became a concern for the German state. This point was emphasized by Chancellor Angela Merkel when she stated in a 2014 speech: "It is our [Germany's] national and civic duty to fight antisemitism" (Kirschbaum and John, 2014). In this way, Germany's efforts to counter antisemitism are motivated not only by self-interest, but also by a moral and ethical remorse for historic crimes against humanity. As the country's approach has developed, the two primary means of responding to this problem have been antiradicalization legal measures and public diplomacy. In the German case, the legal measures are carried out exclusively by the state in a centralized fashion, as law is the domain of the state itself. Public diplomacy, on the other hand, tends to be far more pluralistic, with numerous levels and agencies—both governmental and nongovernmental.

Germany's Legal Approach

Germany's legal approach to antisemitism has tended to focus on three main areas: restrictions on hate speech and incitement (*Volksverhetzung*), adjustments to immigration law, and providing Judaism with legal status on par with major Christian denominations. Each of these areas of policy have been enacted or adjusted since reunification to either counter antisemitic attitudes or work toward reconciliation with the Jewish community.

Hate Speech and Incitement

Article V, Clause I of Germany's Basic Law (Grundgesetz) stipulates the following: "Everyone has the right to freely express his opinions in speech, writing, and pictures" (Bundestag, 2023). However, Article V, Clause II states: "These rights are limited by the provisions of the general laws, the provisions for the protection of young people and in the right of personal honor" (Bundestag, 2023). Therefore, while German law does provide for the freedom of expression, the very next clause states that criminal law may indeed provide limitations. In large part, these restrictions on expression have been enacted to prevent the rehabilitation of Nazism in Germany (Whine, 2008: 61). Additionally, the restrictions have been aimed to prevent the incitement of hatred against Jews and other domestic minorities.

In the German Criminal Code (Strafgesetzbuch), there are two sections that apply directly to restrictions on antisemitic speech. Criminal Code Section 86 makes illegal the "Dissemination of Means of Propaganda of Unconstitutional Organizations." These restrictions apply to any party that has been declared unconstitutional by the Federal Constitutional Court of Germany or "propaganda, the contents of which are intended to further the aims of any National Socialist organization." The statute does, however, provide an exception when such propaganda is used "to promote art or science, research or teaching, reporting about current historical events or similar purposes" (German Ministry of Justice, 2023). Section 86a applies similarly to the use of symbols of unconstitutional organizations. This may include "flags, insignia, uniforms, slogans, and forms of greeting." Penalties for such crimes may include up to three years imprisonment or a fine (German Ministry of Justice, 2023).

The second section that addresses antisemitic and extremist speech in the German Criminal Code is Section 130—Incitement to Hatred. Subsection 1 was introduced in 1960, while Subsections 3 and 4 were added as part of a revision in 1994. The first subsection of the statute, adopted in 1960, is written as follows:

> (1) Whosoever, in a manner capable of disturbing the public peace:
> 1. incites hatred against a national, racial, religious group or a group defined by their ethnic origins, against segments of the population or individuals because of their belonging to one of the aforementioned groups or segments of the population or calls for violent or arbitrary measures against them; or
> 2. assaults the human dignity of others by insulting, maliciously maligning an aforementioned group, segments of the population or individuals because of their belonging to one of the aforementioned groups or segments of the population, or defaming segments of the population, shall be liable to imprisonment from three months to five years. (German Ministry of Justice, 2023)

The third and fourth subsections of the statute apply directly to speech related to Nazism (National Socialism), in particular the issue of Holocaust denial. These sections were added as part of the revision in 1994. The subsections are written as follows:

> 3. Whosoever publicly or in a meeting approves of, denies or downplays an act committed under the rule of National Socialism of the kind indicated in section 6 (1) of the Code of International Criminal Law, in a manner capable of disturbing the public peace shall be liable to imprisonment not exceeding five years or a fine.
> 4. Whosoever publicly or in a meeting disturbs the public peace in a manner that violates the dignity of the victims by approving of, glorifying, or justifying National Socialist rule of arbitrary force shall be liable to imprisonment not exceeding three years or a fine. (German Ministry of Justice, 2023)

It is worth noting that denying the Holocaust specifically was not criminalized in Germany until the revision of Section 130 in 1994. From the language of the statute, Germany offers two primary ways to prosecute those accused of Holocaust denial. Section 130, Subsection 3 makes Holocaust denial a crime as an offense against the public peace, while Subsection 4 considers Holocaust denial a form of libel against the victims (Swart, 2001: 164).

Enforcement of these laws, however, can only be carried out on German territory. As such, the Internet has now become the main source for neo-Nazi and other antisemitic propaganda in the country. Sites are often set up in countries such as the United States or Denmark where the content is not prohibited (Bayzler, 2006: 6). Music has also become a popular means of disseminating antisemitic and racist messaging. Extremist groups and political parties, such as the National Democratic Party (NPD), have been known to distribute music and hold concerts targeting youth to increase support (Deutsche Welle, 2005). The German government has banned over 1,000 songs deemed to be antisemitic or sympathetic to Nazism, but until recently it had been difficult to identify such music on the radio or at rallies and other events. But in 2013, German police developed an app, known as "Nazi Shazam," that allows authorities to recognize banned songs in just seconds via an "audio fingerprint" (Williams, 2013). Nonetheless, developments in technology and an inability to police activity emanating from outside the country present continuing challenges to German authorities in regard to enforcing the legal measures against antisemitism and Holocaust denial.

German-Jewish Immigration Policy

The German Basic Law has had a provision since 1949 allowing for former German citizens and their descendants who were persecuted on political, racial, or religious grounds during the period of Nazi rule to apply to have their German citizenship reinstated. Article 116, paragraph 2 states: "Former German citizens who between January 30, 1933, and May 8, 1945, were deprived of their citizenship on political, racial, or religious grounds, and their descendants, shall on application have their citizenship restored. They shall be deemed never to have been deprived of their citizenship if they have established their domicile in Germany after May 8, 1945, and have not expressed a contrary intention" (Bundestag, 2023).

This provision may, of course, apply to a great number of Jews. In 1990, Germany's estimated Jewish population was about 28,000—a small number compared to the pre–World War II population of 505,000 in 1933 (US Holocaust Memorial Museum, 2023b).

As a response, the German government under the chancellorship of Helmut Kohl created a law in 1991 that allowed Jews from the former Soviet Union to immigrate with few restrictions. In crafting the policy, Kohl met with Heinz Galinski, an Auschwitz survivor who at the time was the chairman of the Central Council of Jews in Germany, and Kohl was sympathetic to the organization's calls to loosen immigration restrictions on former Soviet Jews as a humanitarian gesture and part of an effort to work toward reconciliation with the wider Jewish community (*Der Spiegel*, 1996). Both of these motivations are reflected in the law. Officially, most Jews emigrating from the former Soviet Union were classified by the German government as refugees—hence the humanitarian motivation. However, the loosening of immigration restrictions put Jews on a path to reclaim citizenship similar to that for ethnic Germans from former Soviet states—an equivalency drawn in part to work toward reconciliation (Klusmeyer and Papademetriou, 2013: 192). Despite calls from other government officials to limit the number of Jewish immigrants or impose entry criteria, such measures were rejected. Galinski strongly opposed the entry criteria proposals by arguing, "I, who was exposed to the selection process at Auschwitz, would never give way to [another] selection process" (*Der Spiegel*, 1996). Such arguments were indeed persuasive in shaping German-Jewish immigration policy in the 1990s.

Germany had a Jewish population of 28,000 in 1990, but this number increased to approximately 88,000 by 2000, according to the Central Council of Jews in Germany (Klusmeyer and Papademetriou, 2013: 190). These estimates are, however, based on how the definition of Jewishness is applied. Some estimates placed the population's number at roughly twice that derived by the Central Council (Klusmeyer and Papademetriou, 2013: 190). From 1990 to 2000, Germany received more than 5,000 new Jewish immigrants per year. To help integrate these new populations, the state provided the recently arrived Jewish immigrants with a residence permit, the right to social assistance, housing, and language training (*Der Spiegel*, 1996). Consequently, the German state spent what equates to tens of millions of dollars per year on the program (Cohen, 2000). The reestablishment of Jewish communities in Germany was a goal of Jewish leaders such as Galinski, as well as some German politicians. This was indeed one reason given to justify the costs. Manfred Becker, a senior Berlin city official, stated that, "The reestablishment of a Jewish community is a kind of victory over the Nazis. . . . This is the point, even if such immigration costs money. We feel a sense of moral obligation on the German side" (Cohen, 2000).

However, not all were pleased with the program, and a number of problems began to spark public discussions in the early 2000s. The three major challenges encountered by the arrival of post-Soviet Jewish immigrants can be classified as economic, linguistic, and social.

Given their relatively low birth rate, post-Soviet Jewish immigrants had a higher median age than other immigrant groups. And although their education level tended to be higher than other groups, the Soviet degrees that many had attained often did not translate well to the German system. These factors tended to create difficulty for many post-Soviet Jews, as many found it challenging to find employment commensurate with their qualifications (Remennick, 2005: 35–36). Many post-Soviet Jews also lacked German language proficiency. This provided another hindrance to many in terms of employment opportunities but also led to a certain social alienation. Many post-Soviet Jews lacked regular social interaction with other Germans and instead concentrated social activities in their own networks. These factors often led to the creation of Jewish enclaves in German towns and cities (Klusmeyer and Papademetriou, 2013: 194–195). In essence, these economic, linguistic, and social challenges are all connected and often prevented many post-Soviet immigrants from fully integrating into the German economy and society.

Consequently, the law pertaining to Jewish immigrants to Germany was reformed in 2005. The changes to the law were implemented in order to counter some of the aforementioned problems with integration and the financial burden to the state in the form of welfare payments. Additionally, the Israeli government had been putting pressure on Germany to tighten its immigration laws with regard to Jewish immigration so that more Jews would choose to settle in Israel. In 2004, for example, 20,000 Jews migrated to Germany whereas only 11,000 went to Israel (Bhatti, 2006). For these reasons, Germany enacted a few specific reforms. The changes to the law included requirements that new Jewish immigrants be under forty-five years old, be financially self-sufficient prior to immigrating, and have a good working knowledge of German. These requirements are similar to those for persons wishing to enter Germany for purposes of family reunification or family-forming migration. Jewish immigrants must also show an invitation from a Jewish community in Germany (Klusmeyer and Papademetriou, 2013: 195).

The primary motivation behind opening Jewish immigration was simple: help restore domestic Jewish communities in order to improve relations between Germans and Jews. And while the number of Jews in Germany has drastically increased since 1990, there is no consensus on whether or not the initiative has been successful in achieving the objectives that motivated the policy. Some scholars argue that by treating Jewish immigrants as a special category, this treatment has in effect set the group apart and hindered their overall integration into German society (Klusmeyer and Papademetriou, 2013: 196). Also, given the secularity and mixed heritage of many post-Soviet Jews, many have questioned the authenticity of their Jewish identity (Remennick, 2005: 50). So, while it is clear that the loosening of immigration policy toward Jews in the early 1990s has greatly increased the number of Jews in Germany, debate remains as to whether or not the policy has actually improved German-Jewish relations.

The Legal Status of Judaism

It is important to remember that while Germany has no state church and guarantees for the freedom of religion in Article IV of its Basic Law, the state does in fact play a role in providing support to otherwise independent religious institutions. However, religious institutions in Germany must be considered a legal unit to receive the recognition and support provided by the state in the form of tax benefits and subsidies. In other words, many religious institutions in Germany may engage in partnership with the state to attain certain benefits. Religious institutions may apply to be considered a Public Law Corporation (PLC) under German law, which allows the institution to select chaplains for select state institutions and to levy a tithe (averaging about 9 percent of one's income tax) on its members that is collected by the state (US Department of State, 2023).

For most of the post–World War II period, PLC status was granted to primarily Christian institutions, but in 2003 the German government took a special step to improve relations with the Jewish community. The German government and the domestic Jewish Community (the capital C signifies the distinguishing status of the German Community as a legal unit) entered into a state treaty (*Staatsvertrag*) to officially establish a relationship that would substantially raise the amount of money the Community would receive as a religious institution and provide it legal status similar to that of major Christian denominations (Peck, 2006: 6–7).

The treaty is known as the 2003 State Agreement on Cooperation and was agreed to by both the federal government and the Central Council of Jews in Germany. Germany's Jewish Community had long received financial help from the German federal and state governments, but the 2003 agreement provided an official, legal basis for such subsidies with gradual increases. Federal funding to the Central Council of Jews in Germany increased gradually from 3 million euros in 2003 to

13 million euros in 2018. (Deutsche Welle, 2008; Federal Ministry of the Interior, 2018). The agreement emphasizes that the Central Council of Jews is to support all branches of Judaism with the funds provided. The Central Council reports annually to the federal government on the use of the funds. Additionally, the German federal government provides financial support to Jewish educational institutions, such as the Hochschule für Judische Studien in Heidelberg, the School of Jewish Theology at the University of Potsdam, and the Leo Baeck Institute. The federal government also covers 50 percent of the maintenance costs for Jewish cemeteries in the country (US Department of State, 2023).

Another emphasis of the 2003 agreement was security for Jewish institutions and places of worship. The agreement was officially signed on Holocaust Commemoration Day, and a number of officials, including then-chancellor Gerhard Schröder, condemned all antisemitic acts and vowed to allocate significant resources to investigate such incidents and prosecute the perpetrators (*Haaretz,* 2003). Additionally, the state agreed to provide twenty-four-hour police protection at synagogues and other Jewish institutions (US Department of State, 2023).

The 2003 State Agreement on Cooperation was a transformative step in the relations between the German state and its Jewish population. The agreement legally put Judaism on a status similar to the major Christian denominations, while also emphasizing a degree of partnership between the state and Jewish institutions. The increases in funding to the Jewish Community and related educational institutions may be a contributing factor in reviving modern Jewish life in the country. The emphasis placed on security and the investigation and prosecution by the federal government of antisemitic acts was also a significant step. The actual effectiveness of these efforts is, however, not yet entirely known. The following chapters will seek to address the likely effects that these policy approaches have had over time.

Germany's Public Diplomacy Approach

The Impetus of Collective Guilt

An important impetus behind Germany's response to antisemitism has been the notion of collective guilt—a concept that can be applied both domestically and internationally. Psychoanalyst Carl Jung developed the concept of collective guilt (*Kollektivschuld*) in 1945 and used it to describe a feeling of shame among many Germans for the atrocities committed by their fellow countrymen (Olick and Perrin, 2010: 24–25).

This concept was further brought into the public discourse by the philosopher Karl Jaspers with his 1946 book *Die Schuldfrage*. This feeling of collective guilt was perpetuated in part due to Allied propaganda that carried the slogan of "These Atrocities: Your Fault!" (*Diese Schandtaten: Eure Schuld!*). In this way, US and British occupation forces launched a campaign promoting shame and guilt—a strategy that likely left an impact not only on the German psyche, but also international perceptions of the country (Olick and Perrin, 2010: 109–117).

The notion of collective guilt became a defining aspect of the country's postwar, as well as postreunification, national identity. Mary Fulbrook argues that the impacts of collective guilt are amplified in the German case considering the country's political culture and affective bonds toward collective national identity (Fulbrook, 1999). Lars Rensmann expands upon this point by writing, "If a collective identity (i.e., belief in 'the Fatherland') is highly valued, it may be an especially hard struggle to establish a self-critical political discourse on the country's guilt" (Rensmann 2004: 172). Attitudes and value systems emphasizing a binary friend-foe worldview, antipathy toward Jews, and an exclusionary view of German national superiority are present throughout contemporary German political history; however, as Rensmann goes on to argue, "the post-War social recognition of German guilt and the development of a democratic identity thus had to rely on breaking with essential elements of the German tradition and its conventional narratives" (Rensmann 2004: 172). In other words, for Germany to change perceptions and repair the country's image abroad, the fraught domestic social and political issues relating to the Holocaust and antisemitism needed to be addressed publicly. It is for this reason that one cannot discount the connection between international perceptions and domestic engagement.

Given the extraordinary issues needing to be addressed in the German case, the country's public diplomacy and its development differ from many other Western countries, such as the United States. While many countries indeed have fraught aspects of their history that shape perceptions among others, there are few, if any, events that mark a country's history as deeply and prominently as the Holocaust. Furthermore, the collective identity of many Germans is not only a state issue, but also a very personal and familial issue, given that many contemporary Germans are confronted with atrocities for which their own parents or grandparents may have been responsible. Konrad Brendler developed a typology for how Germans tend to deal with this notion of collective guilt and found a range of emotional responses from defensiveness to shame to ambivalence. Brendler found that 70 percent of Germans born after 1970 had problems wholeheartedly identifying with their German nationality, 65 percent expressed feelings of shame, and 41 percent displayed feelings of guilt. However, some attributed the feelings of shame that they experienced to an undue burden for which Jewish revenge against Germans is responsible, thus perpetuating antisemitic tendencies (Brendler, 1994: 310–315). These factors and the lack of a unified conception of national identity made the development of a coherent and credible public diplomacy campaign especially difficult.

Developing a Public Diplomacy Strategy

A unique aspect of public diplomacy on issues such as antisemitism is the importance of domestic engagement in the process. Much of the literature on public diplomacy focuses on the concept of "promotion" and a country's efforts to emphasize the positive aspects of its culture, political values, and foreign policies. However, events such as genocide can overwhelm international perceptions about a particular country and thus need to be addressed publicly. For international messaging on such issues to be credible, these countries must first demonstrate domestic progress on those issues. As Peter van Ham describes, "branding has become essential to create value in the relationship between territories and individuals" (van Ham, 2008: 128). This relationship, however, is not merely between one territory and populations outside that territory, but also those within the territory. Van Ham goes on to argue that "place branding is also required to make a country's image work for its economy and its citizens" (van Ham, 2008: 128). Such a statement invokes the idea that place or nation branding inherently has a mechanism that is connected to not only external, but also internal, populations. This element of credibility is an important link between the domestic and international spheres. The case of Germany and its public diplomacy efforts regarding antisemitism and the Jewish community is a prime example of this linkage. This section will address Germany's public diplomacy approach on this issue, look at the context and motivations guiding the approach, as well as discuss some of the initiatives that have been implemented.

Although Germany has long placed an emphasis on the cultural and educational aspects of foreign policy, the German conception of public diplomacy has shifted greatly and especially following the end of the Cold War. The totalitarian Nazi regime, while active in promoting its values and culture internationally, allowed little to no room for pluralistic ideas or critical self-reflection—elements central to the credibility of a state's messages. Moreover, the German Democratic Republic (GDR), while not necessarily analogous to the Nazis in their use of state repression, also maintained centralized, nonpluralistic messaging. However, once these governments ceased to exist, so did their goals and messaging (Auer and Srugies, 2013: 21–23). The reunification of Germany in 1990 strengthened the country's place in the world and consequently thrust upon it greater responsibility for cooperation internationally, and especially within Europe.

As a response to Germany's newfound standing and inherent responsibilities, the German Federal Foreign Office (Auswärtiges Amt) developed a strategic document in 1999 called the *Konzeption 2000,* which sought to outline the primary goals and principles of Germany's public diplomacy efforts. The *Konzeption 2000* focused on four main areas: (1) fostering German cultural and educational political efforts abroad; (2) establishing and maintaining a positive modern image of Germany abroad; (3) furthering European integration; (4) preventing conflicts by setting up a dialogue on values (German Federal Foreign Office, 1999). One could argue that the problem of antisemitism and outsiders' perceptions of the problem in Germany undermined Germany's goals in each of these four areas, and it therefore became critical to address them publicly.

Konzeption 2000 was a crucially important document in the formation of Germany's public diplomacy approach and laid the groundwork for numerous programs that have become influential in addressing antisemitism. Notably, much of the document focuses on youth education in collaboration with other countries to inform young people about the crimes and atrocities of the past in order to prevent future violence. One initiative that has been central to this effort has been the Task Force for International Cooperation on Holocaust Education, Remembrance, and Research. The Task Force began in 1998 in cooperation with Sweden, the United States, the United Kingdom, Israel, and Germany. Activities that the task force has undertaken include informational exchanges among students, developing textbooks, and educating teachers on how to discuss the topic of antisemitism with students (German Federal Foreign Office, 1999). This initiative is done in conjunction with other youth exchange, sports, and cultural education programs. The task force and its related activities are a prime example of the connections between the domestic and international realms in Germany's public diplomacy, as well as the efforts to counter antisemitism and cope with issues of the past.

One must note that to develop an effective, credible public diplomacy strategy, Germany needed to go beyond simple public relations and promotional campaigns. An important lesson that policymakers learned from the experiences of the GDR was that honesty and critical self-reflection are necessary ingredients for fostering trust with international audiences (Auer and Srugies, 2013: 22–23). Before a country can effectively and credibly promote itself, its leaders need to have a clear understanding of what is to be represented and how international audiences will most likely respond. Therefore, reunified Germany's public diplomacy campaign required addressing domestic concerns to make international messages credible and salient. As Claudia Auer and Alice Srugies write, "Critical self-reflection also includes reprocessing Germany's past as a precondition for its external representation. . . . Against the backdrop of a growing interconnection of the national and international spheres, this strategy must also apply to domestic audiences" (Auer and Srugies, 2013: 26). While many tend to view public diplomacy as simply a smaller part of a country's larger foreign policy, public diplomacy is indeed closely connected to domestic affairs as well. To develop credible messaging internationally, countries must have a certain consistency between their domestic affairs and the messages they intend to distribute abroad. In other words, the motivations behind the German government's responses to antisemitism are related to both the country's desire to ensure domestic tranquility and its desire to promote a positive image abroad.

Three Layers of Public Diplomacy Actors

It is important to note that unlike with legal measures taken against antisemitism, public diplomacy strategy in the German case is not necessarily centralized within the state. There are a multitude of actors—some governmental, some nongovernmental. The state in many instances, however, does play an important role in agenda setting and facilitation. Auer and Srugies have developed a typology to help explain the various actors in German public diplomacy, and this typology classifies actors as either macro, meso, or micro (Auer and Srugies 2013: 12–15). The typology is displayed in Table 4.1

Macro level. The state itself is considered a macro-level actor given its large amount of resources, funding, and influence. But one must remember that the "state" as a public diplomacy actor is not inherently unified but rather is an aggregation of agencies that may each undertake their own communication efforts. Macro-level actors operate in various sectors of society from military to education to economy. Nonetheless, there

Table 4.1   Actors of Public Diplomacy

Layer	Type	Manifestation	Structure
Macro	Nation as actor	State itself (large government agency facilitators)	Systemic orientation
Meso	Complex actors	Economic or political organizations (parties, interest groups), social and protest movements, companies, private clubs, nongovernmental organizations	Institutional structures
Micro	Individual actors	Role keeper (citizen, organizational role)	Constellation of actors

Source: Auer and Srugies (2013: 15).

are generally certain agencies that take a leading role on certain issues, and regarding antisemitism in Germany the two leading agencies tend to be the Federal Office for Protection of the Constitution (Bundesamt für Verfassungsschutz, BfV) and the Federal Foreign Office (Auswärtiges Amt, AA). The Ministry of the Interior oversees the BfV, and its primary objective is to gather information on domestic threats concerning the country's democratic order—oftentimes extremist groups. The AA is responsible for carrying out Germany's foreign policies, including its relationship with the European Union. Consequently, the structure of Germany's public diplomacy strategy emphasizes this connection between the domestic and international realms. Of course, there are other agencies involved on the macro, governmental level; however, such agencies are often in coordination with, led by, or heavily influenced by the agendas set forth by the BfV or AA.

Meso level. The next, and most complex, level of actors is the meso level. This level consists of a number of societal groups that focus on particular aspects of society, such as politics, culture, or economics (Leonard, Stead, and Smewing, 2002: 8). This includes most non-governmental organizations (NGOs), social groups or clubs, local councils, and even political parties. These organizations and the relationships they forge can have important impacts on the public diplomacy and representations of a country both abroad and domestically. Of course, the goals of these organizations may differ both generally and on particular issues, which demonstrates the decentralized nature of public diplomacy and especially within the German case. Some of the important meso-level organizations in Germany include the Coordination Forum for Countering Antisemitism, Friedrich Ebert Foundation, Konrad Adenauer Foundation, Central Council of Jews in Germany, the Jewish Community of Berlin (Jüdische Gemeinde zu Berlin), and even the major German political parties (such as the Social Democratic Party and Christian Democratic Union). One must note, however, that there are numerous other organizations that may play a role at this level, many of which have relationships with organizations abroad that often participate in financing or the dissemination of messages.

Micro level. The micro level primarily refers to individuals who may lead public opinion or engage in public diplomacy efforts in some way. These may be public figures, such as politicians, artists, or scholars, or even average citizens who exchange ideas with others. In this way, individuals are viewed not only as recipients of public diplomacy messages, but also as communicators themselves. Individuals' actions may be influenced by actors at the macro or meso levels of public diplomacy, but individuals often do act autonomously, which further demonstrates the decentralized nature of public diplomacy—a characteristic evident in the German case. Individuals can engage in public diplomacy through such means as exchange programs, artistic representations, speeches, or any other means intended to represent one's country in some way. Given advances in technology and the increased ability of individuals to communicate internationally, individuals are becoming increasingly important in the exercise of a state's public diplomacy.

Development of Germany's Public Diplomacy Campaign

Initiating public conversations about national identity and complex issues such as collective guilt and antisemitism are indeed lengthy and controversial processes, and this has certainly been the case within Germany. The German word for this process is *Vergangenheitsbewältigung* (coming to terms with the past). The theme of *Vergangenheitsbewältigung* had been prevalent in German culture and discourse for decades, as evidenced by the popularity of the works of such authors as Günther Grass and Siegfried Lenz, and the creation of various museums and monuments dedicated to the victims of the Holocaust and World War II. In 1990, however, the German state recognized that reunification brought along opportunities for Germany to advance its capabilities and leadership role in Europe. Many in German leadership at the time had desires for greater European integration and for Germany to be viewed as a stable element in the West (Katzenstein, 1997: 4). But one of the major obstacles to achieving these goals was the long-lasting damage done to the country's moral authority by the Nazi regime, and particularly the antisemitic violence that many tend to associate with the country and its past. Consequently, the unified German government began to put institutions and messaging in place that not only represent the country abroad, but also facilitate domestic engagement in the process.

Beginning in 1990, Germany's Federal Foreign Office assumed the role of identifying global problems and developing the framework through which Germany's public diplomacy operates. In this way, the AA has acted as a leader in prioritizing the issues upon which the country's messaging and other public diplomacy efforts are based (Rittberger and Wagner, 2001: 16–17). And since 1990, one of the AA's primary goals has been "consolidation of the unity of the German *Kulturnation*" (Karten, 2008: 163). This statement means that the AA sought to integrate the public diplomacy approaches of the Federal Republic of Germany (FRG) and GDR within the structure of the FRG to project the image of Germany as a democratic, trustworthy nation that is defined by its culture. This goal was driven in part by a desire to separate the contemporary, peaceful state from that of the aggressive, violent Nazi past. Consequently, this message draws greater attention to Germany's domestic environment and in some ways invites outsiders to observe closely in what ways the country has progressed beyond the negative aspects of its history.

This desire to demonstrate the country's progress has penetrated numerous areas of its public diplomacy. While the AA was indeed the leading agency in facilitating Germany's early public diplomacy campaign, today's actors are eager to avoid any impressions of replicating the centralized nature of past propaganda ministries (Auer and Srugies, 2013: 25). Consequently, Germany adopted what is known as a "network oriented" strategy to public diplomacy as part of *Konzeption 2000* (Bagger, 2013: 47–48). Under this approach, several federal ministries finance and coordinate public diplomacy efforts, but most activities are carried out by intermediary organizations that operate largely autonomously, such as the Goethe Institute, the German Academic Exchange Service, and the Institute for Foreign Cultural Relations (Auer and Srugies, 2013: 25). This type of approach allows these intermediary organizations to specialize in certain issues and develop domestic and international relationships with other organizations to spread messaging and develop solutions to problems of concern. Notably, the German public diplomacy approach tends to take advantage of the relatively well developed German civil-society organizations in order to amplify messaging both domestically and internationally.

As Germany's approach has developed, there have increasingly been new structures put in place aimed at more effectively coordinating the country's fight against antisemitism. In 2018, Germany established the office of the Federal Government Commissioner for Jewish Life in Germany and the Fight Against Antisemitism. The position was created in order to coordinate the actions of federal ministries more effectively in these areas as well as serve as a liaison between federal agencies, state governments, Jewish groups, and the wider civil society. The Bundestag resolution creating the position states that the commissioner "is to have an independent circle of advisers to be appointed in consultation with the federal government, consisting of Jewish and non-Jewish experts from academia, education and civil society" (Federal Ministry of the Interior, 2023a). A major early initiative of the commissioner's office was to develop the federal government's National Strategy Against Antisemitism and for Jewish Life (NASAS), which was first published in autumn 2022. The NASAS identifies numerous action areas where Germany can improve in combating antisemitism and facilitating a secure environment for Jewish life in the country. These action areas include improving data collection, developing education efforts to prevent antisemitism, fostering a culture of remembrance and historical awareness, establishing punitive measures to respond to antisemitic acts and providing security measures to prevent them, and bolstering Jewish life in the country. The NASAS states that "fostering present-day Jewish life is necessary not only in view of Germany's historical responsibility towards the Jewish community but also in relation to the Federal Republic's liberal democratic basic order" (Federal Ministry of the Interior, 2023b). In this way, the NASAS is aimed to both reconcile with Germany's historical legacy of antisemitism and address future challenges driven by similar forms of hatred.

In addition to these federal initiatives, several German states have taken steps to address antisemitic hatred on a more-localized level. In 2019, the federal state of Berlin established its own strategy to combat antisemitism, which includes a roundtable made up of representatives from government bodies, civil society organizations, and Jewish institutions. In 2021, Bavaria created its own position of antisemitism commissioner and in 2022 adopted a state strategy to combat antisemitism.

In 2022, Schleswig-Holstein appointed a working group to draft its own state plan. Some states that made up the former GDR have also developed initiatives to counter antisemitism. In 2019, Thuringia appointed a law enforcement commissioner dedicated to fighting antisemitism, and in 2021 Brandenburg created a central unit in its public prosecutor's office to deal with hate crimes, which includes a designated person for reporting antisemitic incidents. A few states, including Bavaria, Rhine-Westphalia, and Lower Saxony, have also established agencies to counter hate speech online (Federal Ministry of the Interior, 2023b). These state initiatives, however, largely remain in their infancy as of 2023. Nonetheless, new structures have increasingly been put in place at both the federal and state levels to better coordinate strategies aimed at combating antisemitism in the future.

Major Civil Society Organizations

In addition to the government-led initiatives, there are numerous non-governmental organizations that have been instrumental in forging relationships and delivering the messaging of Germany's public diplomacy campaign against antisemitism. One of the organizations most targeted on this particular goal is the Amadeu Antonio Foundation (AAS), which was established in 1998 and named after one of reunified Germany's first victims of right-wing extremist violence. The AAS has long operated under the patronage of Wolfgang Thierse, a former president of the Bundestag, and has carried out more than 1,700 projects and initiatives aimed at countering antisemitism and racism (Amadeu Antonio Stiftung, 2023b). The AAS maintains a heavy online presence and tends to focus on developing and implementing strategies to counter extremist violence and rhetoric on the local level.

AAS's online initiatives often are collaborative efforts with media and other civil society organizations, with each targeting antisemitism from different perspectives. The AAS operates an online platform called Mut gegen rechte Gewalt (Courage against right-wing violence) in partnership with *Stern* magazine, which chronicles trends in antisemitic violence and proposes strategies to prevent future incidents (Mut gegen rechte Gewalt, 2023). Similarly, the AAS operates the website Belltower News, formerly known as Netz gegen Nazis (Net against Nazis), in partnership with *Die Zeit* newspaper that focuses on reporting the online activities of right-wing extremist groups and contains a database of known extremist group activities in Germany. The staff of this particular website specializes in consulting on how to deal with extremist group members online and in other settings such as the work-place (Belltower News, 2023). As technology develops and extremist groups continually adapt to new technology in their activities, the AAS has worked to develop countermeasures online to oppose the spread of extremist ideology.

Additionally, the AAS has been active at the grassroots level by providing communities with financial, administrative, and expertise support to counter antisemitic and other extremist influences. The AAS is active in opposing neo-Nazi groups in local, state, and national elections through a program called Kein Ort für Neo-Nazis (No place for neo-Nazis). This initiative works to prevent the election of antisemitic and racist candidates to elected office. One of the most prominent examples of the program has been in the state of Mecklenburg-Vor-pommern, where the far-right NPD had won six seats in the state parliament (Landtag) in 2006 and held such seats after the state elections in 2011. That same year, the AAS launched the Kein Ort für Neo-Nazis program within the state in an attempt to ultimately defeat the party and force them out of the Landtag (Linse, 2014). Educational initiatives were launched to counter far-right propaganda, demonstrations were organized, and a Rock Against the Right concert was held to encourage youth to vote and reject the far-right (Amadeu Antonio Stiftung, 2011). The NPD was ultimately defeated in 2016 after receiving only half of their previous vote share and falling below the threshold to receive seats in the Landtag. The AAS continues to operate the Kein Ort für Neo-Nazis program in Mecklenburg-Vorpommern with the stated goal to "prevent the re-entry of the NPD into the state parliament" (Amadeu Antonio Stiftung, 2023a).

The AAS also supports numerous initiatives that promote youth cultures opposed to antisemitism, intolerance, and racism. The goal of these initiatives is to weaken the recruitment prospects of neo-Nazi and other extremist organizations. Finally, the AAS operates a program for victims of antisemitic and other racist violence called the Opferfonds CURA (CURA Victims' Fund). This initiative provides direct support to the victims of extremist violence, informs others about the problems they face, and offers consultations about the best methods for support (Amadeu Antonio Stiftung, 2023c). Through these various initiatives, the AAS has become one of the most active civil society organizations in terms of responding to the problem of antisemitism in Germany.

Another organization that carries out similar work against anti-semitism and extremism is the Center for Democratic Culture (ZDK), which was founded in 1997 with a particular focus on countering extremism in the "new" German states from the former GDR. While the ZDK carries out similar initiatives to the AAS, such as outreach to media, academia, regional governments, and businesses to counter extremist influences, the tactics and emphases of the ZDK tend to differ in some important ways. The ZDK is known for employing "guerrilla tactics" in terms of confronting extremist group members and in their efforts to convince members to leave their particular movements. A prime example of such tactics came in 2012 when the ZDK distributed t-shirts with the words "Hardcore Rebels" at a rock concert known to be popular with extremist group followers. After the first wash, the writing on the shirts would disappear and be replaced with the words "What your shirt did, you can also. We will help you solve right-wing extremism" (Mayer, 2015). The ZDK also organizes a number of marches and organizes counterdemonstrations to those of far-right and neo-Nazi groups (Zentrum Demokratische Kultur, 2023).

Perhaps the most noteworthy of the ZDK's activities is its involvement in the Exit-Deutschland program, which provides a means for far-right and neo-Nazi group members to leave their respective organizations and lifestyles. In fact, one of the cofounders of the program, Ingo Hasselbach, was a former neo-Nazi activist himself. Exit-Deutschland is largely financed by the Federal Ministry of Family Affairs but takes donations from numerous sources (Exit-Deutschland, 2023b). The program helps members of extremist groups who have a desire to leave with counseling and education, and in some instances, security is even provided to those members who have been threatened. The goal of the program is to provide former extremists with personal skills and insight to reorientate their personal relationships and daily lifestyles. In 2013, the German Cabinet made the decision to promote the program long-term and agreed to provide support through at least 2019 (Ostermann, 2013). In October 2019, the Federal Ministry of Family Affairs agreed to financially support Exit-Deutschland on an annual basis thereafter (*Der Spiegel*, 2019). Exit-Deutschland claims to have helped over 800 former extremists overcome their ideologies and leave their organizations from 2000 to 2022, with a recidivism rate of only 3 percent (Exit-Deutschland, 2023a).

Beyond merely combating far-right and other antisemitic groups, German civil society groups, at times in conjunction with governmental agencies, have also been involved in emphasizing the importance of the country's Jewish community and culture. Many of these initiatives are centered in Berlin, which has an estimated Jewish population of between 30,000 and 40,000 (Strack, 2018). One of the most prominent examples of these efforts has been the restoration and reopening of the Jewish Museum of Berlin. The first Jewish Museum of Berlin was founded in 1933 but was closed by the Nazis in 1938. Discussions to construct a new Jewish Museum trace back to the 1970s; however, it was not until 1992 that a cornerstone for the new museum was finally laid (Jewish Museum Berlin, 2023a). The museum's building was completed in 1999 and officially opened in September 2001 with a permanent exhibition entitled "Two Millennia of German Jewish History" that seeks to present Germany through the eyes of the country's Jewish minority. The Academy of the Jewish Museum Berlin was established in 2012 to serve as a forum for discussion in the community on issues of pluralism and the rights of minority populations in Germany (Jewish Museum Berlin, 2023b). The museum has also worked closely with the Leo Baeck Institute and its branches in New York, London, and Jerusalem to promote education on Jewish life in Germany (Foundation of the Jewish Museum Berlin, 2010).

Another organization that has been heavily involved in engaging German Jews with others around the world has been the Jewish Community of Berlin. The Jewish Community of Berlin was established in 1671 but has recently become an active organization in carrying out Germany's public diplomacy messaging, with both governmental and corporate partners sponsoring these efforts. One of the more prominent initiatives has been the Days of Jewish Culture, which began as a cultural festival in Berlin in 1987 but has since spread internationally. Each year, the festivals are dedicated to a different theme and feature theatrical performances, readings, discussions, exhibitions, and concerts from German and international performers, all in an effort to educate the public and build goodwill toward the Jewish community (Jewish Community of Berlin, 2023a). Sponsors of the event have included the Israeli embassy, Mercedes-Benz, the *Berliner Morgenpost,* and Landau Media, among others (Jewish Community of Berlin, 2012).

Another important function of the Jewish Community of Berlin is the group's Integration Office, which was founded in 1998 and seeks to provide support to immigrated Jews in Germany. Approximately two-thirds of the community's members in Berlin are from the former Soviet Union, and the Integration Office provides a number of services to help these individuals adjust to living in Germany, such as job training, sociopolitical and economic education, as well as language training. These initiatives are intended to help German Jews not only obtain employment opportunities, but also take part in social activities and increase communication with other Germans. Additionally, the office provides counseling to those who have difficulty acclimating to life in Germany. The Integration Office provides counseling services to approximately 1,600 German Jews each year in an effort to make the domestic Jewish community feel more comfortable living in Germany (Jewish Community of Berlin, 2023b).

In addition to the public engagement of these civil society groups, other organizations have been established to ensure more consistent documentation and reporting of antisemitic incidents across the country. In 2018, the Federal Association of Departments for Research and Information on Antisemitism (RIAS) was created to aid groups such as the AAS and ZDK in targeting efforts on regional and state levels. The RIAS coordinates with research centers, Jewish groups, and others to establish regional networks that seek to encourage greater reporting of antisemitic incidents by the public, improve upon existing efforts to support victims of antisemitic violence, and advise civil society groups about the nature and extent of antisemitic attitudes and violence in communities. As of 2023, the RIAS is operational in eleven of Germany's sixteen federal states (Federal Association of Departments for Research and Information on Antisemitism, 2023). As the organization continues to develop, the RIAS promises to advance antisemitism research by allowing for more detailed and consistent data collection presenting more accurate representations of the problem within the country.

Conclusion

The German approach to countering antisemitism is certainly multifaceted, involving numerous organizations—both governmental and nongovernmental. The German government has reformed laws regarding hate speech and incitement and immigration laws, and it has engaged in a legal partnership with the domestic Jewish Community to aid in its revitalization. Additionally, Germany has taken a unique approach to public diplomacy by emphasizing self-critical reflection and a decentralized structure to demonstrate the country's progress on the issue of antisemitism. To be sure, the state has played a role in facilitating and financing many of the contemporary efforts, but nongovernmental institutions often specialize in particular areas and establish relationships with other groups inside and outside of the country. Having such a domestic focus in public diplomacy is rare, but antisemitism is one issue where this has nonetheless been the case.

5

Poland Combats Antisemitism

LIKE GERMANY, POLAND HAS INSTITUTED BOTH LEGAL AND PUBLIC DIPLO-
macy measures to counter antisemitism. However, there has been little to
no coordination between these countries in developing their approaches.
In terms of legal measures, Poland has instituted laws against hate
speech, has provided financial support and legal protections to the Jewish community, but has not worked to increase Jewish migration as in the
case of Germany. A unique element of Poland's approach is the establishment of the Institute of National Remembrance, which is tasked with
providing facts regarding "crimes committed against the Polish people"
and prosecuting those who spread misinformation, such as Holocaust
denial (Institute of National Remembrance, 2023a). In terms of public
diplomacy, Poland developed a campaign to combat antisemitism in the
early 2000s as part of a larger effort to build external support for accession to the European Union. However, this campaign has developed over
time to include dialogical forums on Polish-Jewish relations, engaging
Polish and Jewish diaspora groups, and helping rebuild the country's
Jewish culture through the construction of Jewish community centers
and hosting Jewish cultural events.

Since the end of the Cold War, Poland has sought to elevate its
place in the international community but has faced serious challenges to
gaining visibility and addressing perceptions about its controversial
national history. Foremost among those controversial international perceptions was Poland's historical relationship with the Jewish faith. As
the primary location of the Holocaust, Poland has been perceived by
many to be essentially a Jewish graveyard (Ociepka and Ryniejska,

2005: 6). This perception has presented a challenge for Poland in terms of establishing itself as an attractive and credible international partner. To counter these negative perceptions and gain international credibility, Poland has taken legal and public diplomacy steps to demonstrate progress on the issue of antisemitism.

Poland's Legal Approach

Similar to Germany, Poland has adopted legal measures to counter antisemitic behavior, and has indeed done so on many of the same issues as the German government. Poland has passed legislation restricting certain speech on issues such as Holocaust denial, allowed for the repatriation of Poles from the former Soviet Union (many of whom were Jews), and provided support for the primary registered Jewish organization in the country. One must note, however, that Poland's response to antisemitism has developed differently from that in the German case. A primary difference between the two cases is that while the German approach was developed in the midst of reunifying two countries (with West Germany already having some measures in place), Poland was forced to overhaul its entire political and legal system after the fall of communism. This dynamic presented additional challenges in the Polish case and is a likely reason why the Polish approach to antisemitism has in some ways taken longer to develop than in the German case. Nonetheless, both countries have indeed made countering antisemitism a priority in recent times, and while these approaches may differ in terms of their development and timeline, there are certain areas where the approaches overlap and even parallel one another.

Hate Speech and Incitement

Like Germany's Basic Law, the Polish Constitution, adopted in 1997, has provisions intended to protect the right of free expression. Article 14 stipulates that "the Republic of Poland shall ensure freedom of the press and other means of social communication." Similarly, Article 25, Clause 2 stipulates that "public authorities in the Republic of Poland shall be impartial in matters of personal conviction, whether religious or philosophical, or in relation to outlooks on life, and shall ensure their freedom of expression within public life" (Polish Sejm, 2023). These provisions demonstrate the extent to which free expression is codified in contemporary Poland.

However, these rights of free expression do, as is the case in many countries, have limitations. The Polish Penal Code (Kodeks Karny), adopted in 1997, contains provisions regulating hate speech and incitement against social groups based on nationality, ethnicity, race, and religion. Three articles in the Penal Code apply to crimes associated with antisemitism. Article 196 states: "Whoever offends the religious feelings of other persons by outraging in public an object of religious worship or a place dedicated to the public celebration of religious rites, shall be subject to a fine, the penalty of restriction of liberty or the penalty of deprivation of liberty for up to 2 years" (Polish Penal Code, 1997: Article 196). Article 196 can be used to prosecute such crimes as the desecration of religious buildings, cemeteries, and other symbols. Article 256 applies more directly to organized movements advocating for fascist and other totalitarian ideologies that spread hatred against particular groups. Article 256 states: "Whoever publicly promotes a fascist or other totalitarian system of state or incites hatred based on national, ethnic, racial or religious differences or for reason of lack of any religious denomination shall be subject to a fine, the penalty of restriction of liberty or the penalty of deprivation of liberty for up to 2 years" (Polish Penal Code, 1997: Article 256). The third article relating to antisemitic hate crimes is Article 257. Whereas Article 256 focuses on incitement and the promotion of fascist and totalitarian ideologies, Article 257 relates more to the concept of libel against a particular group. In this way, Polish law, like German law, allows for antisemitic rhetoric to be prosecuted as a form of either incitement or libel. Article 257 reads: "Whoever publicly insults a group within the population or a particular person because of his national, ethnic, racial or religious affiliation or because of his lack of any religious denomination or for these reasons breaches the personal inviolability of another individual shall be subject to the penalty of deprivation of liberty for up to 3 years" (Polish Penal Code, 1997: Article 257).

Each of these three articles in the Polish Penal Code allows the state to prosecute individuals for several crimes relating to antisemitism. Article 196 allows for the prosecution of those who desecrate religious symbols or property. Article 256 allows for the prosecution of individuals promoting fascist or totalitarian ideologies that incite hatred against specific national, ethnic, racial, or religious groups. And Article 257 allows for the prosecution against individuals who insult or libel a group based on their nationality, ethnicity, race, or religious affiliation. These provisions are common for legislation relating to hate crimes and demonstrate Poland's understanding of the state interest in such matters.

Although the total number of prosecutions under these laws is unclear, some of the cases related to antisemitic speech have received widespread attention. One of the most significant came in February 2023 when Michał Woźnicki, a priest in the city of Poznań, was convicted of inciting hatred against Jews. Woźnicki gave an online sermon in October 2021 where he said that "Jews in the world have assumed the role of a leech, a tick, a body that lives on the host's body, swells, leading the host's body to death, moving on to the next one" (Klein, 2023). The group Open Republic (Otwarta Rzeczpospolita) reported Woźnicki's statements to prosecutors, who decided to charge him with publicly insulting Jews and inciting hatred based on ethnicity and religious affiliation. The court in Poznań found that Woźnicki violated Article 257 and further set the precedent that giving a sermon does not release a priest from the obligation to obey the law. Consequently, Woźnicki was sentenced to thirty hours of community service per month for six months (*Rzeczpospolita*, 2023). Poland's chief rabbi, Michael Schudrich, stated after the verdict, "The Polish court has handed down a clear verdict that antisemitic hate speech is illegal in Poland. We are hopeful that the Polish courts will continue to find others guilty of this crime" (Klein, 2023).

However, Poland's approach to antisemitism is not limited to the Penal Code. The Institute of National Remembrance (IPN) was founded in 1998 by legislation passed by the Polish Parliament and began operating on July 1, 2000. The IPN's primary mission is to investigate Nazi and communist crimes committed in Poland from 1939 to 1990, but the institute has also been given prosecutorial powers to be exercised against individuals who were either responsible for committing crimes against the Polish nation or individuals who deny the facts of the crimes committed (Stola, 2012). The establishment of this particular institute and its ability to prosecute individuals on issues such as Holocaust denial is a notable element of the Polish approach that is not present in the German case. In essence, the institute is a research organization with special prosecutorial powers.

The IPN's powers are outlined in the "Act of 18 December 1998 on the Institute of National Remembrance"—the legislation establishing the institute. The institute's activities include the investigation and prosecution of crimes relating to both Nazism and communism. Article 1, Clause 1 of the act states that:

Art. 1. The act regulates:
1) the recording, collecting, storing, processing, securing, making available and publishing of the documents of the state security author-

ities, produced and accumulated from July 22, 1944, until July 31, 1990, as well as the documents of the security authorities of the Third Reich and the Soviet Union relating to:

a) the Nazi crimes, the communist crimes, other crimes against peace, humanity or war crimes, perpetrated on persons of Polish nationality or Polish citizens of other nationalities between September 1, 1939, until July 31, 1990. (Institute of National Remembrance, 2023a)

In short, Article 1 outlines the scope of the institute's research activities. The IPN's prosecutorial powers are stated later in Article 55, which states, "Anyone who publicly and contrary to the facts denies crimes referred to in art. 1, point 1 shall be subject to a fine or the penalty of imprisonment of up to 3 years. The sentence shall be made public" (Institute of National Remembrance, 2023a). While Article 55 may be vague in terms of what speech can be prosecuted, certain types of antisemitic speech, and particularly Holocaust denial, can be viewed as denial of Nazi crimes and thus can make one the subject of prosecution.

The IPN is divided into eight parts, each of which is responsible for carrying out a portion of the institute's mission. The two parts most of concern in terms of the legal measures regarding antisemitism and Holocaust denial are the Bureau of Provision and Archivization of Documents and the Chief Commission for the Prosecution of Crimes Against the Polish Nation (Institute of National Remembrance, 2023b). The Bureau of Provision and Archivization of Documents is most responsible for determining the facts relating to Nazi and communist crimes against the Polish people (including Jews) and the Chief Commission for the Prosecution of Crimes Against the Polish Nation is responsible for not simply prosecuting those who committed such crimes, but also those who deny the crimes. In this way, this centralizes the investigation and prosecution of such offenses within a single institute and is a primary difference between how the German and Polish governments approach issues of Holocaust denial and antisemitic speech.

The IPN did, however, become a point of controversy in 2018 when the ruling Law and Justice party proposed a new law entitled the Amendment to the Act on the Institute of National Remembrance. Perhaps most controversial was Article 55a, which stated that "whoever claims, publicly and contrary to the facts, that the Polish Nation or the Republic of Poland is responsible or co-responsible for Nazi crimes committed by the Third Reich . . . or for other felonies that constitute crimes against peace, crimes against humanity or war crimes, or whoever otherwise grossly diminishes the responsibility of the true perpetrators of said crimes—shall be liable to a fine or imprisonment for up to 3 years" (*Times of Israel,* 2018a). The law also amended the IPN's mission statement to include "protecting the reputation of the Republic of Poland and the Polish Nation" (*Times of Israel,* 2018a). Such legislation marked the most prominent reforms of the IPN since its creation.

Consequently, the 2018 law received widespread international condemnation, particularly from Israel and the United States. Yad Vashem (the World Holocaust Remembrance Center) released a statement arguing the law "is liable to blur the historical truths regarding the assistance the Germans received from the Polish population during the Holocaust" (*Times of Israel,* 2018b). Similarly, the American Jewish Committee wrote in a statement opposing the law that "while we remember the brave Poles who saved Jews, the role of some Poles in murdering Jews cannot be ignored" (American Jewish Committee, 2018). Numerous Polish leaders, including former president Aleksander Kwaśniewski and former minister of foreign affairs Radosław Sikorski, signed a statement criticizing the law and asking, "Will the testimony of a Jewish survivor who 'feared Poles' be a punishable offense? . . . Is this law intended to be symmetrical to the law forbidding Holocaust denial?" (*Guardian,* 2018). Despite these concerns and condemnations, the law was enacted on February 6, 2018, although a later revision removed the possibility of criminal prosecution for such offenses but still allowed for fines in civil court. While the 2018 law did not officially alter the existing responsibilities of the IPN to research Nazi and communist crimes and prosecute offenses such as Holocaust denial, its drafting seemed to restrict the IPN's ability to fully investigate and report historical findings and some argue even created a chilling effect on discussions of antisemitism within Poland.

To summarize the legal measures against antisemitism in terms of each countries' penal code, Poland and Germany have similar laws relating to hate speech and incitement against Jews and other societal groups. Each country has laws against incitement, libel, and the promotion of fascist or totalitarian symbols. The unique aspect of the Polish approach is the role of the IPN. Poland delegates prosecutorial powers on matters of antisemitism to multiple agencies. Given its focus on historical research and documenting Nazi and communist crimes, the IPN is the agency tasked with prosecuting crimes such as Holocaust denial, whereas the Polish Ministry of Justice and local prosecutors are tasked with prosecuting other offenses relating to incitement, libel, and violence. So, although Poland and Germany may have some notable differences in how crimes relating to antisemitism are investigated and prosecuted, both countries have nonetheless adopted laws against hate speech, incitement, and Holocaust denial.

Polish-Jewish Immigration and Repatriation

Similar to Germany, Poland has enacted laws allowing for the repatriation of citizens and their descendants who were displaced for reasons of deportation, exile, and persecution—reasons that affect a number of Jews with Polish roots. However, Poland has not taken the additional steps that Germany has with regard to treating Jews as a special category of refugees. In fact, the historical persecution of religious minorities is not specifically mentioned in Polish immigration and repatriation law as it is in the German case. Instead, Poland makes "persons of Polish extraction" the sole category for repatriation with the same standards for all applicants, regardless of factors such as religious affiliation (Polish Ministry of the Interior, 2023).

The Polish Constitution states in Article 52, Clause 5 that "anyone whose Polish origin has been confirmed in accordance with statute may settle permanently in Poland" (Polish Sejm, 2023). This statement is quite broad and does not provide a specific definition of "Polish origin." To clarify this provision, the Polish government passed the Repatriation Act of November 9, 2000. This act has consequently become the primary law governing the repatriation of Polish citizens and their descendants persecuted under Nazism and communism.

The stated goal of the act is to recognize that "the duty of the Polish State is to allow the repatriation of Poles who had remained in the East and in particular in the Asian part of the former Union of Soviet Socialist Republics and due to deportations, exile and other ethnically-motivated forms of persecution could not settle in Poland" (Polish Ministry of the Interior, 2023). The act further goes on to describe the criteria necessary for one to be declared of "Polish extraction." Article 5 of the act declares that to qualify for repatriation one must have at least one parent or grandparent or two great-grandparents of Polish nationality, as well as "demonstrate links with Polish provenance, in particular by cultivating Polish language, traditions and customs" (Polish Ministry of the Interior, 2023). While these laws do not refer to displaced Polish Jews in particular, they do nonetheless provide a path for Polish-Jewish Holocaust and other victims, as well as their descendants, to return to the country.

While Poland does indeed have laws allowing repatriation for those displaced due to Nazi and communist persecution, it is notable that Poland has not targeted such laws toward Jews, as Germany has, in order to rebuild domestic Jewish communities. Whereas Germany's Jewish population was estimated to have tripled from 1990 to 2000, in part due to the loosening of immigration restrictions on Jews, Poland did not experience similar growth. Estimates of the Jewish population in Poland since 1990 have consistently remained anywhere from 3,200 to 10,000 depending on the source (Jewish Virtual Library, 2023; Yivo Institute for Jewish Research, 2023a). Of course, Poland did not explicitly state the revitalization of Jewish communities through immigration as a state goal, as was the case in Germany, and the laws tend to reflect this difference. This is not to say that Poland has not placed an emphasis on revitalizing domestic Jewish communities, but it is worth noting that the Polish approach to antisemitism and efforts toward reconciliation with the Jewish community prioritizes Jewish immigration and repatriation to a lesser extent than in the German case.

Legal Status of Judaism in Poland

While contemporary Poland is overwhelmingly Catholic, the concept of religious freedom is emphasized in the Polish Constitution and has been throughout much of the country's history. Article 53, Clause 1 of the constitution states, "Freedom and conscience of religion shall be ensured to everyone" (Polish Sejm, 2023). As of 2019, there were approximately 190 faith groups and religions registered with Poland's Ministry of Interior and Administration, and although registration is not necessary to practice one's religion, registration does provide these denominations with certain legal protections and benefits regarding taxation (Central Statistical Office of Poland, 2020; US Department of State, 2022). The primary Jewish organization in the country is the Union of Jewish Religious Communities in Poland, which was officially registered in 1993, and is a continuation of the earlier Religious Union of Judaism established in 1946 (Adam Mickiewicz Institute, 2023). And although Polish law does not explicitly prioritize any denomination over others, the place of Judaism in the country is an issue that tends to receive significant attention.

Although Poland does not have a similar tax program to Germany, whereby parishioners contribute directly to their denomination via taxation, the government does nonetheless provide some resources and funding to religious institutions, including Judaism. The Ministry of Culture is the primary state funding source to the Jewish community in Poland and has supported several projects through the Union of Jewish Religious Communities in Poland (Adam Mickiewicz Institute, 2023). Most prominent among these involvements has been state funding and other support of the Foundation for the Preservation of Jewish Heritage in Poland. The foundation is the "only institution in Poland officially dedicated to the task of recovering, preserving, and commemorating physical sites of Jewish significance" (Foundation for the Preservation of Jewish Heritage in Poland, 2023). The organization's main task is the restoration of the physical representations of Poland's Jewish community, such as synagogues, cemeteries, and other markers. An example of state funding for these efforts occurred in 2016 when $26,000 was earmarked in the Ministry of Culture's budget to be used toward renovations of an eighteenth-century synagogue in Przysucha (Jewish Heritage Europe, 2016). Although such funding has been modest and not made on a consistent basis, the Polish government has nonetheless demonstrated a state interest in preserving Jewish religious and cultural sites within the country.

The largest single investment by the Polish government to support a Jewish institution was its contribution to the Museum of the History of Polish Jews (POLIN). Construction of the building began in 2009 with the Ministry of Culture and City of Warsaw contributing $45 million of the total $100 million construction costs (Polish Ministry of Culture, 2009). State officials played a visible role in establishing the museum, with then-president Lech Kaczyński laying the museum's cornerstone. The museum sits on a site within the former Warsaw Ghetto and includes multimedia exhibitions and numerous artifacts of cultural and historical significance to the country's Jewish community covering approximately 1,000 years of history. The museum officially opened in April 2013 and by 2022 had over 2 million visitors (POLIN Museum, 2022). In 2016, the museum was awarded the European Museum of the Year Award from the European Museum Forum (Jewish Telegraphic Agency, 2016). Although the museum serves as an institution of Jewish culture and history and is not necessarily in and of itself a religious institution, the state funding for the project has demonstrated a level of state commitment in supporting the preservation of Jewish history and culture domestically.

One particularly controversial public policy issue regarding antisemitism in Poland has been that of restitution for past persecution. Many countries in Europe have taken to addressing the issue of restitution, but given that Poland until World War II had the world's largest Jewish community, the issue is amplified in this case. Restitution can be made for different reasons, including losses of personal property, losses of communal property, and personal harm. Poland has laws regarding restitution on some issues but lacks such laws on others.

Poland remains the only country in the European Union with no law requiring private property confiscated by the Nazis, or later nationalized by the communists, to be returned to families or for the family to be compensated for such property. Since 2001, there have been at least six bills in the Polish Sejm proposing private property restitution, but these bills have either not passed or have been vetoed by the executive (World Jewish Restitution Organization, 2023). The failure to pass such legislation has received criticism from numerous Jewish organizations, especially the World Jewish Restitution Organization, and even Polish officials such as former president Bronisław Komorowski, who in 2011 argued that the lack of a private property restitution law was "a disgrace for Poland" (Ain, 2015). With the lack of such legislation, the Polish government's official position is that private property claims should be dealt with through normal channels in the Polish courts—an often time-consuming, complex, and expensive process (World Jewish Restitution Organization, 2023). Consequently, the issue of private property restitution remains a controversial public policy topic and point of tension between the Polish government and several Jewish organizations.

Nonetheless, while Poland does not have restitution laws regarding private property, the government has passed legislation and created agencies to deal with the restitution of communal property—such as synagogues, cemeteries, and other buildings serving religious, educational, cultural, and social purposes. The Law on the Relationship Between the State and Jewish Communities was passed in 1997 and governs the restitution of Jewish communal properties within the country. As part of these efforts, the state also established the Polish Government Commission on the Restitution of Jewish Property, which has an equal number of officials from the Polish State Treasury and the Union of Jewish Communities. The Commission is the primary body responsible for adjudicating claims of Jewish communal property in Poland. The Foundation for the Preservation of Jewish Heritage also partakes in the process by organizing and submitting claims. As of 2022, there were 5,504 claims submitted by Jewish communities; however, only about half of those claims have been reviewed, and of those less than half have received a positive decision or were settled by agreement (World Jewish Restitution Organization, 2023). Moreover, many of the claimed properties are in serious disrepair, the costs of which are by law to be covered fully by the property owner. This issue, while directly involving officials from both the state and the Union of Jewish Communities and having legislation enacted to govern the process, also remains a controversial point of tension between the state and numerous Jewish institutions.

Nonetheless, it is also worth noting that Poland has enacted legislation to compensate victims of the Holocaust who were Polish citizens at the time. In 1991, the Polish government empowered the Office for War Veterans and Victims of Oppression to provide benefits to any Polish citizen who had been in a death, concentration, labor, or transit camp; in hiding; or persecuted during the subsequent Soviet occupation until 1956. However, the program received criticism from several organizations, including the World Jewish Restitution Organization, because many victims no longer resided in Poland and thus did not have a Polish bank account—a requirement to legally receive the compensation. Consequently, the law was amended in 2014, eliminating this requirement and allowing a greater number of Holocaust victims of Polish origin to claim benefits. The amendment has allowed tens of thousands of additional victims to claim benefits of approximately $135 per month. Sebastian Rejak, Poland's former Special Envoy to the Jewish Diaspora, has stated that "ethnic criteria are irrelevant, but we acted with a special sensitivity for the Jewish survivors of the Holocaust" and added "Jewish victims have to be looked at with special attention when we talk about World War II—that goes without saying. Their legal status is the same—it's a question of sensitivity and reaching out" (Ahren, 2014). So, while contemporary Poland has not legally treated Jews as a group distinct from other Poles, there have indeed been some special measures taken with regard to the country's Jewish community of past and present.

Poland's Public Diplomacy Approach

Poland's public diplomacy did not necessarily begin as a response to antisemitism, but the issue of antisemitism has nonetheless become a central issue affecting both foreign and domestic perceptions of the country. The original impetus for launching a public diplomacy campaign was Poland's desire in the late 1990s and early 2000s to achieve EU accession. However, survey data determined that antisemitism and the legacy of the Holocaust were the foremost image among other Europeans about Poland (Ociepka and Ryniejska, 2005). Such data helped craft a public diplomacy campaign that has over time made Polish-Jewish relations a central point. Consequently, Poland—and especially the governmental ministries leading the campaign—has over time fostered relationships with Jewish organizations domestically and abroad to demonstrate progress on the issue.

One must note that contemporary Poland does not have the level of civil society development that is observed in the German case, in large part due to the history of Soviet communist oppression in the country. Therefore, Poland often tends to forge partnerships with organizations based outside the country. Given Poland's comparatively large diaspora population, this has in many ways been a convenient and cost-effective approach. But beyond this, Poland has also emphasized outreach to Jewish communities and organizations, largely because there are few more credible messengers to represent Poland's progress than Jews themselves. By fostering such relationships, one could say that Judaism has increasingly been reincorporated as part of contemporary Poland's national brand. So, while the German case highlighted a number of non-governmental organizations that work to counter antisemitism directly, the Polish case tends to be defined by the government's efforts to incorporate Judaism into Poland's national brand—a message targeted not only to foreign audiences but domestic as well. Poland's means of addressing antisemitism through public diplomacy have tended to emphasize not simply targeting far-right and other antisemitic groups, but rather focusing on promoting positive connections between Poles and Jews and the contributions that Jews have made to Poland—both historically and in the present.

The Early Focus—Correcting Mischaracterizations

Like Germany, Poland emerged from the Cold War era seeking to improve its global standing. Poland had numerous economic, political, and social challenges in its postcommunist transition that were different from the German case, and this dynamic is likely a key reason why Poland's responses to antisemitism developed comparatively later. Nonetheless, Poland was conscious of outside perceptions and the impacts of antisemitism and the Holocaust on the country's reputation. This became especially apparent as the country's efforts to achieve EU accession increased.

In a 2000 public opinion survey of western European countries, only 44 percent of respondents supported the idea of Poland's accession to the European Union. While this percentage was higher than for some other postcommunist countries, such as Romania (34 percent) and Bulgaria (36 percent), it was nonetheless shy of a majority (Euro-barometer, 2000). There were naturally a variety of reasons why some may have disapproved of this prospect; however, what Polish officials found most concerning were attitudes and misperceptions regarding

Poland's role in World War II and accusations of antisemitism (Ociepka and Ryniejska, 2005).

Extensive content analysis also revealed one of the likely factors contributing to such attitudes and accusations was the language used by media sources in western Europe, such as "Polish concentration camps," "Polish death camps," or "Polish gas chambers." Such statements were found not only in popular media, but also in academic textbooks. A study of western European textbooks found that phrases such as "Polish antisemitism" and "Polish discrimination against Jews" were commonly used without adequate mentions of Nazi occupation or figures representing the number of Polish casualties in concentration camps and uprisings. Many sources also commonly failed to distinguish between the 1943 Warsaw Ghetto Uprising and the 1944 Warsaw Uprising or make adequate mention of the coordination between Jewish and Polish resistance forces in either instance (Kulczycki, 2005). Responding to these perceptions, and what many would consider mischaracterizations, became an important task for Polish authorities considering the majority of western Europeans had never been to Poland and their perceptions and attitudes were largely shaped by secondhand experiences, media coverage, and information from schools or informal groups (Ociepka and Ryniejska, 2005). Indeed, one of the primary purposes of public diplomacy is to respond to controversial accusations and attitudes toward a particular country, and those pertaining to Polish-Jewish relations are a prime example of the sort of questions and misperceptions that require a response.

Initially, Poland's public diplomacy efforts lacked coordination between governmental agencies and were greatly challenged by a relatively low budget and lack of communications resources. Efforts aimed to counter negative perceptions were largely handled by the Ministry of Foreign Affairs, and to a lesser extent by the Ministry of Culture. Nonetheless, with the establishment in 2002 of the "Program for the Promotion of Poland in the EU During Ratification of the Accession Treaty," the Ministry of Foreign Affairs gradually became the leading agency in public diplomacy efforts with a great deal of the program decentralized and decisions being made by the individual embassy in each target country (Ociepka and Ryniejska, 2005). These early public diplomacy efforts became known as the "Framework Program," which is an apt description because it only began to lay the framework for the future, more-coordinated efforts that would eventually follow.

In May 2004, once Poland had attained EU accession, the Ministry of Foreign Affairs continued the public diplomacy campaign and began adopting a more coherent message and brand for the country after consulting with brand specialist Wally Olins. Olins believed that Poland's brand ought to invoke the message that "Poland is part of the West and also understands the East" (Ociepka and Ryniejska, 2005). Given the historical undertones of Olins's brand message, Poland was provided an ideal opportunity to determine what constitutes modern Polish identity and how negative foreign perceptions could best be addressed.

Polish-Jewish relations remained a central concern that required a coherent response. One of the ways in which the Ministry of Foreign Affairs has provided such a response has been by addressing the perpetuation of mischaracterizing language in media, including the terms "Polish death camps" and "Polish gas chambers." In 2005, Polish Foreign Minister Adam Daniel Rotfeld claimed that instances of such phrases being used has been in "bad will, saying that under the pretext that 'it's only a geographic reference,' attempts are made to distort history and conceal the truth" (Zychowicz, 2005). The Polish government also began appealing to international organizations to aid in their attempts to counter mischaracterizations of Polish history. In 2007, the Polish government filed a request with the United Nations Educational, Scientific, and Cultural Organization (UNESCO) to change the official name of "Auschwitz Concentration Camp" to "Auschwitz-Birkenau" with the subtitle of "German Nazi Concentration and Extermination Camp (1940–1945)" to put greater emphasis on the Nazi German origins of the camp. UNESCO's World Heritage Committee agreed to approve the request (UNESCO, 2007). Additionally, the Ministry of Foreign Affairs created a webpage entitled "Against Polish Camps" that attempted to chronicle instances in which media sources used such phrases and to consequently demand corrections. Countering media reports has indeed been an important aspect of promoting a renewed Polish identity abroad, but it has by no means been an effort done in isolation.

Creating a National Brand

The development of concise messages and images to improve a country's reputation is an element, or one may say a new method, of conducting public diplomacy. Nation branding is closely related to commercial branding because both aim to attract support for a particular product, which in the case of nations can be their culture, political ideals, or policies. However, to develop a coherent national brand, a nation's citizens must also be actively involved in developing and promoting the brand, because if they are not, the brand will likely lack credibility. For public diplomacy to be effective, it must have credibility or else risk reverting to mere propaganda. As Joseph Nye explains, "Simple propaganda often lacks credibility and thus is counterproductive as public diplomacy" (Nye, 2008: 101). For this reason, Poland's Ministry of Foreign Affairs adopted a more cooperative approach that involved not only governmental agencies, but also NGOs, religious institutions, and other elements of the emerging Polish civil society.

In some ways, Poland actually benefits from being a medium-sized country with a relatively homogenous population, in that it becomes more able to establish a national brand with expediency compared to larger, more diverse countries such as Germany. Because of its size and the particular international concerns regarding the Polish nation, Poland is more able to narrow its focus on specific issues to address and incorporate into a coherent and concise brand. Since 1989, Poland has attempted to shed perceptions of its communist social identity previously imposed by the Soviet Union. Carrying on since the end of the Cold War and emerging in 1978 with the election of Pope John Paul II, Poland has largely been defined by a Catholic identity that along with elements of the Solidarity movement has continued to the present day. Until the beginning of its public diplomacy in 2000, however, the Polish government had not coherently projected such a national identity abroad, but since it has done so this identity has evolved and come to include additional elements that previously remained questioned by outsiders. In order to incorporate these elements, there needed to be certain domestic developments for the promoted image or brand to remain credible. For this reason, there have indeed been linkages between Poland's public diplomacy and Polish domestic society.

Current Public Diplomacy Strategies

In the early stages of its public diplomacy campaign, particularly within the Framework Program, Poland's target audiences were primarily opinion leaders and others with foreign policy influence. However, as the campaign developed, it increasingly reached out to the mass public as well. As was mentioned, there was little coordination between governmental agencies, much less nongovernmental organizations, in Poland's early public diplomacy efforts. But this has not been the case since the Ministry of Foreign Affairs has taken a greater lead in embracing public diplomacy as an international strategy. Dialogical efforts that brought together the aims of the Ministry of Foreign Affairs and NGOs were not an initial emphasis of Poland's public diplomacy, but as the program progressed, coupled with an increased emphasis on nation branding, a more cooperative approach was adopted.

A common tactic to amplify messages abroad has been to engage diaspora groups and perhaps groups with which a state has a connection but may have lost contact for a variety of reasons. Poland was ripe to make diaspora outreach a part of its public diplomacy strategy given its diaspora population (meaning people of Polish ancestry) of approximately 20 million, a population just over half of its own 38 million (Polish Ministry of Foreign Affairs, 2023a). Furthermore, given the questions surrounding Poland's history and relationship with the Jewish faith, there are few more credible and capable of representing Poland's progress and respect for the Jewish community than members of the community themselves. For this reason, outreach to Jewish organizations and communities has become an important aspect of Poland's public diplomacy and national branding that has not diminished, but rather has built upon its postcommunist Catholic and Solidarity infused national identity.

Outreach efforts that the Ministry of Foreign Affairs have undertaken to embrace Jewish groups include cultural and academic exchanges, conferences to promote dialogue, participation in Jewish cultural events, as well as a conscious campaign to counter the attitudes of those who may hold antisemitic views. Remarkably, as its national brand has gradually become an important component attempting to tie different aspects of Poland's public diplomacy together, engagement in a variety of activities has been more apt to promote a coherent message, as opposed to the less-cohesive public diplomacy previously carried out by individual embassies. Even as public diplomacy efforts tend to be led by governmental figures and agencies, in many cases NGOs and even individuals play an important role in communicating and exercising "soft power" both internationally as well as domestically.

Until 2008, the Polish government did not explicitly use the term "public diplomacy" but rather referred to "promotion." This changed, however, when the department responsible for promotion of the country within the Ministry of Foreign Affairs was renamed the Department of Public and Cultural Diplomacy in 2008. These efforts were accelerated in 2009 when Polish law was amended to establish public diplomacy as one of the primary missions of the Ministry of Foreign Affairs (Ociepka, 2012). These developments, while important in terms of officially establishing public diplomacy as a strategy of Polish foreign policy, were in fact a culmination of efforts that more closely coordinated efforts between governmental and nongovernmental organizations.

Since its public diplomacy campaign began, the Polish Ministry of Foreign Affairs has regularly held forums for increased dialogue among Polish officials, Jewish leaders, and other civil society leaders both inside and outside Poland. These forums have increased in frequency as the campaign has developed, particularly since the Department of Public and Cultural Diplomacy was established, and by 2016 the Ministry of Foreign Affairs held approximately three or four per month (Polish Ministry of Foreign Affairs, 2023b). The topics of the forums have varied but commonly reflect themes promoting certain aspects of Polish national identity. In many cases, the forums have been held in honor of individuals who represent historical connections between Poles and Jews. Some of those around whom forums have been organized include Irena Sendler, Jan Karski, and Witold Pilecki—all members of the Polish resistance known for aiding Jews during the Holocaust. Events honoring these figures have become common at Polish missions abroad and have been a central theme attempting to unite Poles and Jews, as well as create international partnerships to help enhance Polish-Jewish relations worldwide.

Moreover, one of the first sections in a 2012 report by the Ministry of Foreign Affairs chronicling public diplomacy efforts and plans was entitled "Polish-Jewish Dialogue." The Foreign Ministry emphasized the importance of these efforts by stating, "Symmetric dialogue in Polish–Jewish relations is an essential part of the Polish public diplomacy. This important communication tool is used not only by governments, but also in the public spheres of individual states, whose important components are Jewish NGOs and institutions, as well as opinion-making circles within the Jewish diaspora" (Polish Ministry of Foreign Affairs, 2012). Events have included Jewish film festivals and educational programs, particularly in Israel. Through these efforts, Polish officials have attempted to embrace the Jewish elements of Poland's national identity in order to obtain partnerships to help further Poland's soft power influence abroad and consequently have strengthened Jewish organizations' reach inside Poland.

Although it has substantial influence in Polish society and is often associated with Polish identity, the Catholic Church has played only a limited role in the country's public diplomacy and fight against antisemitism. The Catholic Church has engaged in interfaith dialogue through such organizations as the Vatican's Commission for Religious Relations with the Jews; however, these organizations tend to be more inclined to emphasize positive theological ties between faiths rather than engage directly with the public to dispel myths and counter discrimination. Nonetheless, Pope John Paul II specifically did take steps to promote better relations between Catholics and Jews and work toward reconciliation. John Paul II became the first pope to visit Auschwitz-Birkenau in 1979, make an official visit to a synagogue in 1986, and visit Yad Vashem in 2000. He also gave a speech at the Western Wall in Jerusalem where he said, "I assure the Jewish people the Catholic Church . . . is deeply saddened by the hatred, acts of persecution and displays of antisemitism directed against the Jews by Christians at any time and in any place," while also adding that there were "no words strong enough to deplore the terrible tragedy of the Holocaust" (BBC News, 2000). Such words carry special significance coming from a Polish pope who had lived much of his life fewer than a hundred miles from Auschwitz-Birkenau.

More recently, the Catholic Church has furthered some of Poland's public diplomacy goals by promoting positive historical connections between Catholic and Jewish Poles. One such incident came in September 2023 when the Catholic Church took the unprecedented step of beatifying an entire family of nine Catholic Poles, including a newborn baby, who were killed in 1944 by German military police for sheltering a Jewish family. Pope Francis wrote in a letter about the beatification, "We authorize that from now on the venerable Servants of God, Józef and Wiktoria Ulma, spouses and their seven children . . . (who) fearlessly sacrificed their lives for the sake of love for their brothers and welcomed into their home those who suffered persecution, be given the title of blessed" (CNN, 2023). Schudrich, Poland's chief rabbi, said of the beatification, "We have an obligation to remember the righteous and have them as role models of who we want to be" (CNN, 2023). Such a message is in many ways consistent with the wider Polish public diplomacy campaign.

Nonetheless, critics often claim that the Catholic Church has not been sufficiently vocal in condemning antisemitism with regularity. Stanisław Krajewski, cochair of the Polish Council of Christians and Jews, has argued that the Catholic Church's silence has allowed antisemitism to fester within Polish society. Krajewski has stated, "It would help the Jewish community if the church said something, and if those now seeking to join Catholicism with antisemitism are properly rebuked" (*National Catholic Reporter,* 2018). Some socially conservative outlets in Poland, such as Radio Maryja, are known to use Catholicism to spread antisemitic views. Although numerous Catholic leaders have raised concerns about such outlets, Radio Maryja has the seventh most listeners of any radio station in Poland and registered a 3 percent share of total listening time in the country from February to April 2023 (Puhl, 2006; Bylok and Pędziwiatr, 2010; Kozielski, 2023). This dynamic allows some Catholic nationalists to undermine many of the more conciliatory messages from the Catholic Church and provides a significant challenge to Poland's wider public diplomacy strategy.

Attempts to Revive Domestic Jewish Culture

Dialogue between Polish officials and Jewish communities has notably increased through formal events and partnerships that have in large part grown through public diplomacy. These efforts have been focused on Jewish groups both abroad and domestically. Some international exchange agreements have existed since the mid-1990s but have substantially increased as public diplomacy has become more organized. Forums for discussion have been held with far greater regularity ever since Polish-Jewish relations became a core element of public diplomacy. These efforts together have indeed contributed to an increased emphasis on Jewish culture within Poland.

It is worth noting that one of the first initiatives to create an international Polish-Jewish partnership began even before Poland's efforts regarding EU accession, although the program's influence has increased as the Ministry of Foreign Affairs and partner organizations have expanded the public diplomacy campaign. The bilateral agreement of the Forum for Dialogue Among Nations with the American Jewish Committee began in 1996 to create partnerships between Polish and Jewish leaders and achieve mutually beneficial goals (Forum for Dialogue Among Nations, 2023). Polish officials initially viewed the program as beneficial in terms of strengthening Poland's relationship with the United States in its efforts to attain NATO membership, and Jewish leaders became able to renew relationships with government officials and Jewish leaders in the nation that once had the world's largest Jewish population.

While not originally part of a larger, cohesive public diplomacy campaign, the Polish-Jewish Exchange Program has evolved into an important part of Poland's recent public diplomacy campaign by reaching out to important audiences with which Poland had lost much contact during the Cold War period—Jewish communities (both domestically and internationally) and Polish diaspora in the United States. In recent years, the program has put a spotlight on Poland's relationship with the Jewish community and recruited more high-profile participants. Since 2000, the program has included ministers, ambassadors, Jewish intellectuals, and journalists. One of the most notable participants was Władysław Bartoszewski, Poland's former secretary of state, foreign minister, and an Auschwitz survivor. The exchange as a whole has encouraged greater cooperation between Poles and Jews but has also notably encouraged foreign opinion leaders to become involved within Poland's Jewish community and in many ways foster its revitalization.

Poland has also been expanding its network of Polish-Jewish exchanges with Israel, which has led to such events as the Polish Year in Israel 2008–2009. This particular event included involvement from Poland's Ministry of Culture, the Polish Institute in Tel Aviv, the Israel Philharmonic Orchestra, and other cultural institutions. From March 2008 to June 2009 over 260,000 spectators attended 140 events in twenty locations. The Polish Ministry of Culture deemed the Polish Year in Israel a success as it claimed that one in twenty Israeli adults had encountered Polish culture during the project and more than 1,500 media stories covered the events (Polish Ministry of Culture, 2023).

There is evidence that this sort of increased Polish-Jewish dialogue internationally has led to greater international funding and attention directed toward Poland's domestic Jewish community. Perhaps one of the largest and most influential Jewish organizations in twenty-first century Poland has been Krakow's Jewish Community Center, which was created directly through connections and funding acquired through public diplomacy. During a 2002 visit to Krakow, then prince Charles of the United Kingdom met with Jewish leaders in the Kazimierz District and learned that Krakow's Jewish community did not have a meeting place outside of individual synagogues. After the meeting, Prince Charles personally vowed to help secure funding for a Jewish center in the city to help bring Krakow's Jewish community together (Jewish Community Center of Krakow, 2022). Prince Charles's involvement helped draw attention to the cause and compel World Jewish Relief and the American Jewish Joint Distribution Committee to also help raise funds and contribute resources. In November 2006, ground was broken on the $3.5 million center. The project was completed in April 2008 with Prince Charles and the Duchess of Cornwall formally opening the center (Jewish Community Center of Krakow, 2022).

Since Krakow's Jewish Community Center has opened, it has become an attraction for Jews, non-Jews, and tourists to come together and learn about Jewish culture and participate in Jewish cultural events, holidays, and other traditions. As of July 2017, there were 630 active members of the center, which considering the estimated Jewish population in Poland of only 3,200 to 10,000 is substantial (Baumol, 2017). However, membership is not a condition for participation in activities run by the center; in fact, it has been routine for the center to leave its doors open to any who desire to enter (Baumol, 2017). Krakow's Jewish Community Center is an important cultural institution that has been influential in the revival of Jewish life in the country, but it has also been complemented by other instances of public diplomacy having an effect on Poland's Jewish communities.

One of the most visible examples of the Jewish revival has been in Krakow with noticeable increases in attendance and funding for the annual Krakow Jewish Culture Festival. The festival began in 1988 when twenty-eight-year-old Janusz Makuch, a collector of films about Israel and traditional Jewish music, decided to gather with friends from the local Jewish community at Krakow's Mikro movie theater for a film screening and series of lectures. In its early years, the event lacked funding and could only be held every other year. However, Poland's Ministry of Culture eventually discovered the public diplomacy potential of the event and began offering funding to make the event an annual affair (Tzur, 2013). Since then, the festival has gradually added donors and partner organizations, and in 2009 it began organizing year-round workshops, presentations, and concerts. The festival itself is held annually in June with approximately 30,000 people attending, a remarkable number, more than Poland's entire Jewish community population (Baur, 2022). The 2013 budget for the festival reached $1 million, with most contributions coming from the Polish government and international Jewish organizations—a partnership strengthened through public diplomacy initiatives (Tzur, 2013). These efforts have been amplified through media coverage, as the final open-air concert of the festival known as "Szalom on Szeroka Street" is televised live on national television, and the event is now customarily held under the patronage of the president of the Republic of Poland. It is also worth noting that the Jewish Community Center of Krakow has become one of the chief partner organizations for the festival (Zubrzycki, 2012: 447). For these reasons, the festival has received international attention and has begun accepting donations from the Swiss government, Goldman Sachs, and other international entities, consequently drawing international attention to progress in Polish-Jewish relations and helping move beyond the negative perception of Poland representing a Jewish graveyard (Jewish Community Center of Krakow, 2022).

Jewish cultural festivals have, however, not been limited to Krakow. By 2012, there were some sixteen Jewish cultural festivals in thirteen cities throughout Poland (Zubrzycki, 2012: 447). Krakow has nonetheless become the center of the recent Jewish revival with other organizations being created and building off the success of the cultural festival. Beit Krakow—a progressive Jewish group led by Poland's first female rabbi, who came to the country via Israel in 2007 with the intent of helping revive the Jewish community—has held over five hundred of its own cultural and religious events celebrating contemporary Jewish life in Poland since 2009. Beit Krakow has invited international performers to visit and present classic Hebrew texts to contemporary audiences through music, dance, and theater (Jarosz, 2013). Performers have visited from countries such as Israel and Russia. These partnerships have helped to serve Poland's public diplomacy goals by providing credibility to the image projected internationally of a vibrant Jewish community.

Interestingly, these events have not been targeted exclusively toward Polish Jews but more generally toward anyone with an interest in Jewish culture. In fact, a 2007 report estimated 85 percent of attendees at the Krakow cultural festival to be non-Jews (Schaechter, 2007). This increased popularity of Jewish culture has also led to increases in Jewish businesses as Poland has become increasingly commercialized. Before World War II, Jewish cafés and markets were a common sight throughout Poland, but after decades of Nazi and communist rule, this was no longer the case. In the early 1990s, Krakow's historically Jewish Kazimierz District had no businesses with roots in Jewish culture or tradition. The first Jewish café opened in 1992 but had little indication of any other Jewish themed establishments in the surrounding area in the years following. This changed, however, as the Jewish Culture Festival has gained in popularity. By 2012, there were over a dozen Jewish establishments in the Kazimierz District alone (Grollmus, 2012). Some have questioned the authenticity of such establishments since many owners are in fact non-Jews and many Jewish cafés are nonkosher. Although this may be the case, the fact that embracing Jewish culture is not only an initiative undertaken by a few elites but also a popular and commercial success indicates an improvement between Poles and Jews and in the outside perceptions of the Polish-Jewish relationship.

Some have argued that the increased emphasis on common Polish-Jewish history and the conscious efforts to establish Judaism as an element of Polish national identity has been merely an attempt by progressives to introduce pluralism into a country that is 96 percent ethnically Polish and 95 percent Catholic (Zubrzycki, 2012: 444). Indeed, there has been some backlash from conservative nationalists who point to Poland's homogeneity as a reason to implement conservative social policies. However, this has not universally been the case. In fact, one of the most elaborate projects undertaken to emphasize Polish-Jewish commonalities began under the leadership of the conservative Law and Justice party. The decision to create Warsaw's POLIN museum was made in 2005, with the cornerstone for the building being laid in June 2007 by then-president Kaczyński of the Law and Justice party.

The Ministry of Culture and City of Warsaw, at the time also led by a Law and Justice government, each contributed toward the 43,000-square-foot building's construction on the edge of Warsaw's former Jewish Ghetto, with an additional $40 million being raised by international NGOs to finance the museum's exhibitions (POLIN Museum, 2023). Exhibitions feature multimedia content about the historical vibrancy of Poland's Jewish community, covering over 1,000 years of Jewish contributions to Polish society. Additionally, the museum is being complemented by an online project called the "Virtual Shtetl," which launched in 2009 and offers Polish-English websites that list maps of 1,240 Polish towns with statistics and picture galleries providing information on Jewish life in Poland prior to World War II and the Holocaust (POLIN Museum, 2023). Such initiatives are consistent with the common theme throughout Polish public diplomacy of emphasizing positive contributions that Jews have historically made to Polish society and the role they have played in shaping the country's identity.

Although the POLIN museum's creation was largely a unified effort among Poland's political class, tensions began to arise about the museum's mission since the Law and Justice party was able to form a majority government in 2015. These tensions are most clearly exemplified in the government's decision in 2019 to replace historian Dariusz Stola as the POLIN museum's director. Stola served as director from 2014 and was due to be reappointed after receiving eleven of the fifteen votes from the nominating committee as well as the endorsement of two of the museum's founding partners, the City of Warsaw, and the Association of the Jewish Historical Institute. However, the minister of culture, Piotr Gliński, refused to confirm the nomination (Grisar, 2020). Critics argue that Gliński's decision was due to Stola's opposition to the 2018 law amending the Institute of National Remembrance, which sought to make claims of Polish assistance during the Holocaust illegal, as well as the existence of museum exhibits depicting post–World War II antisemitic persecutions and antisemitic quotes from individuals linked to the Law and Justice party (Plucinska, 2020). Stola has since joined other former museum directors in complaining of increased political interference since Law and Justice came to power in 2015. Stola has claimed that "a large part of the ruling party's efforts aim to sweep unpleasant things under the rug, and this is a distortion of history" (Plucinska, 2020). So, while institutions such as the POLIN museum have worked to demonstrate common connections and improve relations between Poles and Jews, complaints about political, and specifically Law and Justice, interference have recently called into question the government's motives and direction in addressing issues of antisemitism in Polish history and society.

Conclusion

Poland's response to antisemitism shares some similarities with the German approach, with a few notable differences. Both countries have laws prohibiting Holocaust denial and certain antisemitic speech, but Poland's establishment of the Institute of National Remembrance with its prosecutorial powers provides an additional means of countering antisemitic speech. The Polish government has also publicly and financially supported numerous Jewish cultural, social, and even religious institutions—albeit via direct funding as opposed to the German approach of levying taxes on parishioners. Nonetheless, controversy remains about inconsistent and complex policies regarding restitution for Polish Jews who suffered historical persecution.

Poland's public diplomacy campaign has had less of a focus on addressing and confronting antisemitic groups directly and more of a focus on fostering positive relationships with Jewish organizations and emphasizing to the wider public the positive contributions the Jewish community has made to Poland. The initiatives for spreading such messaging have involved bilateral exchange agreements, supporting Jewish institutions and events, and supporting educational initiatives through centers such as the POLIN museum. Poland does not have the level of NGOs and other initiatives to directly confront antisemitic groups and parties that is observed in the German case; instead Poland has placed greater emphasis in its messaging on incorporating Jewish life into Poland's modern identity in a manner that appeals to Polish Jews and non-Jews alike. These efforts have been aimed at emphasizing cooperation between these groups for the purposes of both countering domestic antisemitism and projecting a tolerant image and brand of the country abroad. These initiatives and themes have been the defining characteristics of Poland's approach to antisemitism. So, while Germany and Poland have similar goals in mind with regard to addressing the problem of antisemitism, there are indeed some notable differences in terms of the measures taken and development of the approach.

6

Evaluating
Germany's Efforts

IN LOOKING AT HOW EFFECTIVE GERMANY'S STRATEGIES HAVE BEEN IN
countering the problem of antisemitism, I evaluate the trends over time
of a number of indicators: membership in far-right groups, election
results for far-right political parties, antisemitic attitudes, crimes and
violent attacks, and perceptions of antisemitism from the domestic Jewish community. Analyzing this data allows for a better understanding of
the areas where these policies have been most and least effective. Particularly important to note are changes in the data following policy
implementation. As explained in previous chapters, the first policies
implemented in reunified Germany were increasing Jewish immigration
(1991) and a ban on Holocaust denial (1994). The public diplomacy initiatives in Germany were launched following the publication of *Konzeption 2000* by the Federal Foreign Office in 1999. Shortly thereafter,
Judaism was granted full legal status and increased benefits from the
German government in 2003. This timeline of policy implementation is
important with regard to the analysis in this chapter.

The Influence of Far-Right Groups

As was mentioned in Chapter 4, many of the German legal and public
diplomacy responses to antisemitism focus on countering far-right
extremist groups. Groups classified as far-right include neo-Nazis,
skinheads, and certain political parties, such as the National Democratic Party of Germany (NPD), Die Republikaner, the former German

People's Union (DVU), and other groups with similar ideologies. As will be demonstrated later, those with a far-right ideology are responsible for approximately 91 percent of all antisemitic crimes and 83 percent of violent antisemitic attacks. Consequently, countering these groups has been a top priority of the German response to antisemitism. Germany's Federal Office for Protection of the Constitution tracks membership in such groups and releases the data via annual reports on extremism. Figure 6.1 graphs these membership data.

This figure shows that membership in far-right groups reached its peak in the early 1990s and has generally declined since that time. These data indicate that efforts to counter far-right groups have been effective in terms of decreasing membership and the ability of such groups to recruit new members. This decrease is especially notable after 2000—the year in which Germany's public diplomacy campaign was launched. It was also around this time that civil society organizations, such as the Center for Democratic Culture (ZDK) and Amadeu Antonio Foundation (AAS), were established and began implementing strategies to counter the influence of the far-right. Prior to 2000, far-right group membership tended to be quite volatile, but since that time the data has shown an overall decline in membership. Around 2014, membership in German far-right groups decreased to approximately one-third of its

Figure 6.1   Membership in German Far-Right Groups (1991–2022)

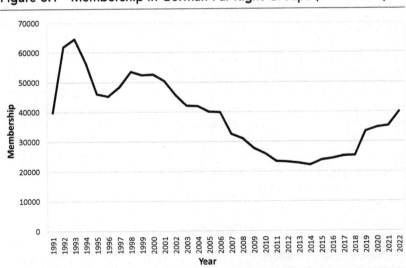

Source: Federal Office for Protection of the Constitution (various years).

high point in 1993. While it is true that membership in German political parties overall also declined over this period—with an average decline of 27 percent from 1993 to 2014—far-right groups experienced a 66 percent decrease over the same period (Niedermayer, 2016: 2). This discrepancy indicates that there are likely additional factors influencing the sharp declines in far-right group membership. Particularly since these declines were sharpest after the year 2000, it is likely that public diplomacy initiatives were a contributing factor. Nonetheless, from 2014 to 2022 there has been a substantial increase in the membership of such groups from 22,150 in 2014 to 40,000 in 2022—an 81 percent increase. This increase indicates that there has been substantial regression in the success of these efforts.

However, while the data show that membership in far-right groups in reunified Germany remain at lower levels than in the 1990s, this has not been the case regarding the success of far-right parties in national and local elections (see Figure 6.2).

Until 2013, the two major German far-right parties were the NPD and Die Republikaner. From 1990 to 2013, aggregate electoral support for these two parties in national Bundestag elections remained between 1 percent and 2.5 percent. And while Die Republikaner declined in

Figure 6.2 Bundestag Election Results for Far-Right Parties (1990–2021)

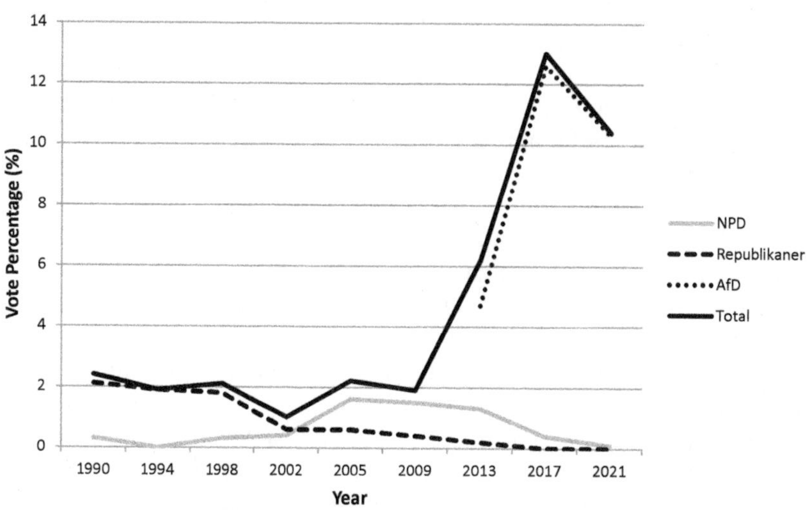

Source: Wahlrecht.de website (2023).

national electoral support after 1990, the NPD largely gained support until about 2005. Yet, since German reunification, neither party achieved the requisite 5 percent of the vote necessary to obtain seats in the Bundestag. However, with the establishment of the Alternative for Germany (AfD) in 2013, far-right politics became more mainstream and electorally successful. The AfD received 4.7 percent of the vote in 2013, just 0.3 percent shy of the 5 percent threshold needed to obtain seats in the Bundestag, but in 2017 the party received 12.6 percent of the vote, clearing the threshold and becoming the third-largest delegation in the legislative body.

While running on a platform of German nationalism and anti-immigration policies, the AfD has sought to capitalize on the anxiety of many Germans regarding policies ranging from the eurozone crisis to an influx of refugees fleeing violence in Syria. However, elements of the party have been accused of exploiting antisemitism as well. For example, Björn Höcke, one of the founders of the AfD, was quoted as stating in a 2017 speech in reference to the Berlin Holocaust Memorial, "Germans are the only people in the world who plant a monument of shame in the heart of the capital" (Chambers, 2017).

To differentiate themselves from other far-right parties such as the NPD and Die Republikaner, the AfD has claimed the support of German Jews and embraced a group known as Jews in the AfD. One of the primary reasons for this shift from other far-right parties is likely that it enables the AfD to shield itself from accusations of antisemitism and create a broader base of support. As Rogers Brubaker argues, "They can remain marginal and appeal to a limited sector of the electorate, or they can try to become mainstream and overcome barriers that prevent other parties from cooperating with them" (Samuel, 2018). This has ostensibly been a more successful approach given that the AfD has achieved electoral success unattainable by the NPD and Die Republikaner. Cas Mudde adds to this point by arguing that parties such as the AfD "use philo-Semitism to appear more moderate, or not radical right, given that the radical right is still very much associated with antisemitism in Europe" (Samuel, 2018). In further attempting to shield itself from accusations of antisemitism, the AfD has contended that modern antisemitism is not so much a problem of the far-right, but rather Germany's growing Muslim population. This argument aligns with the party's anti-immigrant platform and allows the AfD to frame itself as not an adversary of the country's Jewish community but rather an ally. This messaging centered around Islamophobia and ethnocentrism has been successful in attracting a certain segment of Germany's Jewish population; however, there are no exact numbers available because political parties do not collect data on their members' religious affiliation (Nicholson, 2018). As Brubaker contends, "Anti-Muslimism has become a very successful master frame for radical-right, anti-immigrant parties throughout Europe in the last 15 years. The logic is that the enemy of my enemy is my friend" (Samuel, 2018). So, while the AfD may align with other far-right parties in their platforms and rhetoric, the AfD has also developed new ways to shield itself from accusations of antisemitism and appear more mainstream, achieving electoral successes that have eluded other like-minded parties. And despite the AfD vote declining to 10.4 percent in 2021, the party still maintained its substantial presence in the Bundestag.

Although neither the NPD nor Die Republikaner achieved national representation in the Bundestag, there have been two state legislatures where the NPD has been successful in winning seats. The NPD was able to break the 5 percent threshold necessary for representation in the Saxon Landtag in 2004 and the Mecklenburg-Vorpommern Landtag in 2006, as shown in Table 6.1.

In 2004, the NPD achieved its largest electoral victory in reunified Germany winning 9.2 percent of the vote and gaining twelve seats in the Saxon Landtag election. The party then lost support in subsequent elections, losing four seats and only earning 5.6 percent of the vote in 2009.

Table 6.1 NPD Landtag Election Results

	Saxony			Mecklenburg-Vorpommern	
Year	Percentage of Votes	Seats		Percentage of Votes	Seats
1990	0.7	0		0.2	0
1994	0	0		0.1	0
1998				1.1	0
1999	1.4	0			
2002				0.8	0
2004	9.2	12			
2006				7.3	6
2009	5.6	8			
2011				6	5
2014	4.95	0			
2016				3.02	0
2019	0.61	0			
2021				0.8	0

Source: Wahlrecht.de website (2023).

Table 6.2   AfD Landtag Election Results

	Saxony		Mecklenburg-Vorpommern	
Year	Percentage of Votes	Seats	Percentage of Votes	Seats
2014	9.7	14		
2016			20.8	18
2019	27.5	38		
2021			16.7	14

Source: Wahlrecht.de website (2023).

Then in 2014, the party was unable to reach the 5 percent threshold and consequently lost its representation in the Landtag, with its vote declining since. In Mecklenburg-Vorpommern, the NPD experienced a sharp rise in support to 7.3 percent of the vote in 2006 from 0.8 percent in the previous election in 2002. The party subsequently won six seats in the Landtag in 2006 before declining to five seats in 2011 and then falling below the threshold since.

While the NPD's vote share has declined at the state level, the AfD has inversely experienced far more electoral success over that same period. Table 6.2 shows the electoral success of the AfD in Saxony and Mecklenburg-Vorpommern—the two states where the NPD previously held seats—since its founding in 2013. In fact, the AfD's success goes far beyond these areas, with the party having held seats in every Landtag as of 2022 (Wahlrecht.de website, 2023). The AfD's rise has been particularly noteworthy in Saxony where it has quickly become the second-largest party, nearly reaching a plurality with 27.5 percent of the vote to the Christian Democratic Union's 32.1 percent in 2019 (Wahlrecht.de website, 2023). These results are notable because while the AfD may not be as overtly antisemitic as the NPD, the AfD has nonetheless taken far-right politics mainstream, including many antisemitic elements (Salzborn, 2018).

These data indicate mixed results regarding the success of German policy and public diplomacy approaches to countering far-right groups and political parties. While overall membership in such groups has largely declined since 1990, and the overtly antisemitic NPD has declined in its vote share, the rapid rise of the populist, far-right AfD since its founding in 2013 presents a new challenge. Additionally, while the number of members in far-right groups remains below the levels of the 1990s, there was an 81 percent increase in membership between 2014 and 2022. Therefore, the data suggest that while some progress has been made since reunification, 2014 became a turning point as the far-right has since gained strength both in terms of group membership and electoral success.

Antisemitic Attitudes

In addition to evaluating the many German efforts to counter antisemitism that are focused on far-right groups, it is also important to evaluate their effectiveness with regard to the general German population. As noted in Chapter 4, Germany has attempted to demonstrate progress on the issue of antisemitism through its public diplomacy messaging. In order to do so, these efforts have required a substantial amount of domestic engagement, both with NGOs and governmental agencies. Numerous programs and legal measures have been adopted to facilitate such engagement and reduce the influence and prevalence of antisemitic ideologies and attitudes. Although there has not been a reliable and consistent survey tracking data on antisemitic attitudes in Germany since 1990, Leipzig University in conjunction with the Heinrich Böll Foundation has been collecting such data since 2002. The survey data from these organizations does not provide a complete picture of antisemitism since reunification but nonetheless does provide insight regarding recent trends. On the topic of antisemitism, respondents are asked whether they agree with the following three statements: "Even today, the influence of Jews is too great," "The Jews use dirty tricks more than other people to get what they want," and "There is just something special and peculiar about the Jews and they don't quite fit in with us." A respondent agreeing to all three statements is classified as manifestly antisemitic (Decker et al., 2022). Figure 6.3 displays these survey results from 2002 to 2022 for those classified as manifestly antisemitic while also noting the differences in attitudes between the states of the former East Germany and West Germany.

The data show that manifestly antisemitic attitudes in Germany as a whole have decreased gradually since 2002, falling from 9.5 percent in 2002 to 3.2 percent in 2022. These trends tend to mirror the data in Figure 6.1 (that showed membership in far-right groups) until 2014—at which point far-right group membership began increasing yet general attitudes continued to decline. Notably, antisemitic attitudes have decreased in both the states of the former West Germany and the former

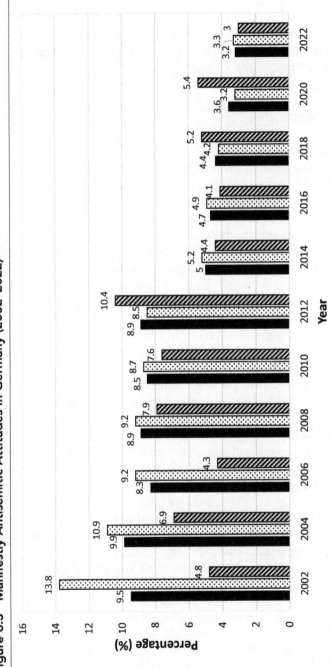

Figure 6.3 Manifestly Antisemitic Attitudes in Germany (2002–2022)

Source: Decker et al. (2022).

East Germany over the twenty-year period measured. Levels of manifest antisemitism have declined from 13.8 percent in 2002 to 3.3 percent in 2022 in the western states and decreased in the eastern states from 4.8 percent in 2002 to 3.0 percent in 2022. Such results indicate that the German initiatives to counter antisemitism have been effective in reducing such attitudes among the general German population over this time period.

It is, however, notable from Figure 6.3 that prior to 2012 antisemitic attitudes in the eastern states (although more volatile) had been lower than in the western states. These data would seem counterintuitive considering the electoral successes and relative strength of the NPD and other far-right parties and groups in the states of the former German Democratic Republic. However, one likely explanation for this seeming discrepancy is that antisemitism may not be the primary motivating factor for individuals to join far-right groups or vote for far-right parties. The same study conducted by Leipzig University also asked respondents whether they agreed with the following statements: "The foreigners only come here to take advantage of our welfare state," "When jobs become scarce, foreigners should be sent back to their homeland," and "The Federal Republic is overwhelmed by the many foreigners to a dangerous degree" (Decker et al., 2022). The data in Figure 6.4 show the percentages of those who answered they agree with all three statements and are therefore classified as manifestly xenophobic.

Figure 6.4 shows that although the states of the former East Germany may have had lower levels of antisemitism prior to 2012, these states also tended to have higher levels of xenophobic attitudes than western Germany and the general German population. This dynamic may help to explain the relative successes of far-right parties in this region of the country. While antisemitism is certainly a common element in many far-right parties and groups, it may not be as prevalent of a motivation as xenophobia for those who decide to join or vote for such parties and groups. Levels of xenophobic attitudes have shown to be many times more prevalent in each category than antisemitic attitudes over the same time period. However, given that approximately 90 percent of German Jews are also immigrants, there may indeed be an area of overlap between antisemitic and xenophobic attitudes (Ben-Rafael, 2015: 57). Xenophobia and antisemitism are also often connected via conspiracy theories such as the white replacement theory, which asserts that wealthy Jews are responsible for financing mass migration for the purpose of changing the demographics of countries with large white, Christian populations. Consequently, hatred directed toward members of Germany's

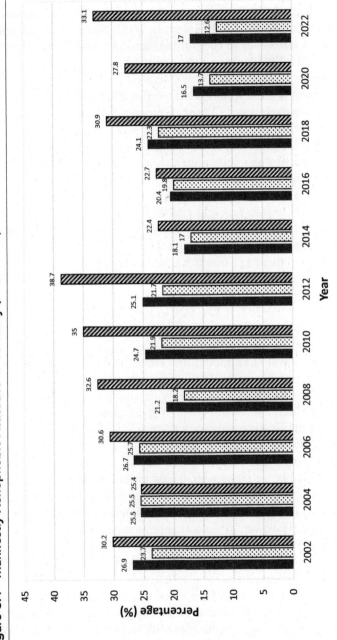

Figure 6.4 Manifestly Xenophobic Attitudes in Germany (2002–2022)

Source: Decker et al. (2022).

Jewish community may not be entirely antisemitic, as the prevalence of xenophobic attitudes may also lead to hatred and discrimination toward members of the community.

Although data on the subject has not been collected consistently, survey research has shown that antisemitic attitudes have tended to be higher among Germany's Muslim population than the general or Christian populations. A 2006 survey conducted by Pew Research showed that 44 percent of German Muslims viewed Jews either very unfavorably (31 percent) or somewhat unfavorably (13 percent). These levels were higher than for the general German population, in which 22 percent viewed Jews either very unfavorably (5 percent) or somewhat unfavorably (17 percent) (Pew Research Center, 2006). Another survey in 2013 showed similar results in which 28 percent of German Muslims stated they could not trust a Jewish person compared to 10.5 percent for German Christians (Jikeli, 2015). It is not possible to demonstrate a trend with these data, given that the questions asked differ, but the results do indeed demonstrate a difference regarding religious antisemitism in Germany. The data suggest that the German responses to antisemitism tend to have less salience in terms of reaching and influencing the country's Muslim population.

Antisemitic Attacks and Crimes

Another important indicator of antisemitism is the prevalence of attacks and crimes committed with an antisemitic motive. As described in earlier chapters, Germany has adopted certain hate crimes legislation regarding antisemitism (first adopted in 1960 and expanded in 1994), and the Ministry of the Interior maintains data on the number of antisemitic violent attacks and overall antisemitic crimes committed. Behavior intended to physically harm another person or persons are considered to be violent attacks, whereas the data representing total antisemitic crimes includes violent attacks, hate speech, and intentional damage to property. Figure 6.5 represents violent antisemitic attacks in Germany from 1991 to 2022, and Figure 6.6 represents the total number of antisemitic crimes over the same time period.

As Figure 6.5 shows, the number of violent antisemitic attacks in Germany has not followed a linear trend. The number of attacks recorded tended to be lower in the 1990s and fluctuated thereafter until reaching high points from 2018 to 2022. One potential explanation for the relatively low number of violent antisemitic attacks during the

110

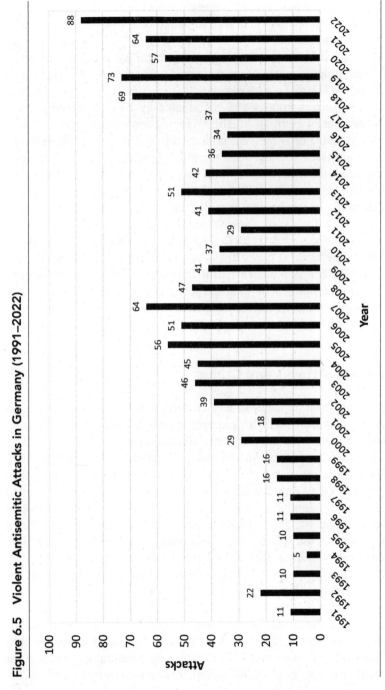

Figure 6.5 Violent Antisemitic Attacks in Germany (1991–2022)

Source: German Ministry of the Interior (various years).

Figure 6.6 Antisemitic Crimes in Germany (1991–2022)

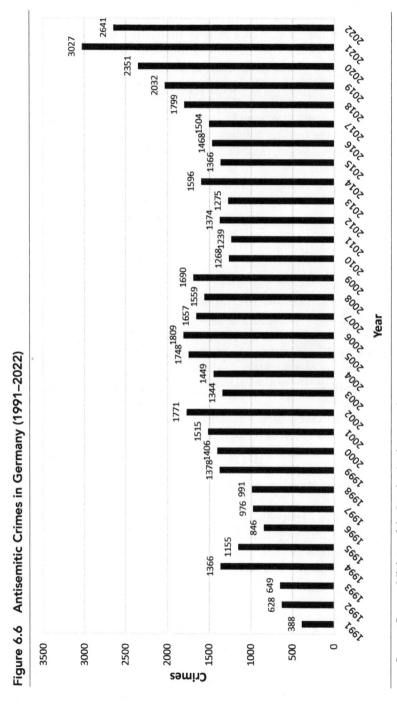

Source: German Ministry of the Interior (various years).

1990s is that the Jewish population in Germany was much smaller than in the years since 2000. According to the Central Council of Jews in Germany, the country's Jewish population tripled from 28,000 in 1990 to 88,000 in 2000 (Klusmeyer and Papademetriou, 2013: 190). Consequently, since 2000 there have simply been more German Jews who could be potential victims of attacks. A second possible explanation is that external events may lead to increased attacks in particular years. Controversy over foreign policies, particularly with regard to Israel, as well as other economic, political, social, religious, and other developments all have the potential to stoke the primary manifestations of antisemitism that have long played a role in Germany's history and affairs. A third possible explanation is that the strategies to counter antisemitism have not been consistently successful in preventing violent attacks. One could argue that there was some success in reducing antisemitic attacks from 2007 to 2017; however, such efforts certainly have not been as successful in the years since.

To paint a more complete picture of levels of antisemitism, it is also important to examine the overall number of antisemitic crimes over time. The numbers in Figure 6.6 include violent antisemitic attacks, but also those crimes involving hate speech and damage to property. The data show that only about 2.6 percent of all antisemitic crimes since 1991 are violent attacks against others; the vast majority of antisemitic crime is categorized into the latter categories of hate speech and damage to property.

The statistics on total antisemitic crimes in Figure 6.6 seem to resemble those on violent attacks. Both indicators were relatively lower but increasing during the 1990s, generally declined from 2007 to 2017, but then increased to new highs after 2018. Similar to Figure 6.5, a rise in the domestic Jewish population, the role of external events, and an inability of strategies to consistently prevent antisemitic crime each serve as possible explanations for the trends revealed by the data in Figure 6.6. What this empirical evidence suggests is that while the percentage of those holding antisemitic attitudes may have shrunk in size (Figure 6.3), the motivation of those willing to engage in radical actions and crime did not weaken. This recent rise in crime received international media coverage with the 2019 shooting targeting a synagogue in the city of Halle, which resulted in the deaths of two nearby, non-Jewish individuals. The Halle attack received increased attention in large part due to the shooter live-streaming the attack online—a recent trend in far-right attacks around the world (Eddy, Gladstone, and Tsu, 2019). This particular attack was also significant in demonstrating to the wider

German society the common dangers of antisemitic violence to both Jews and non-Jews alike.

Beyond the aggregate crime numbers, noting the perpetrators of such crimes is important to understand the trends more fully. Germany's Ministry of the Interior has collected such data since 2002 and releases the numbers in the agency's annual reports on politically motivated crime. Table 6.3 shows the data relating to violent antisemitic attacks, and Table 6.4 reports the total numbers for antisemitic crimes committed.

According to the data in Table 6.3, right-wing ideologies were responsible for 83 percent of all violent antisemitic attacks between 2002 and 2022. Left-wing ideologies only accounted for 1.2 percent of all violent attacks, and perpetrators of what are classified as foreign ideologies account for approximately 11.5 percent. These data demonstrate

Table 6.3   Violent Antisemitic Attacks by Perpetrator in Germany (2002–2022)

Year	Violent Antisemitic Attacks	Right-Wing	Left-Wing	Foreign Ideology	Other
2002	39	30	1	7	1
2003	46	38	0	7	1
2004	45	40	1	3	1
2005	56	50	1	3	2
2006	51	44	0	7	0
2007	64	61	0	3	0
2008	47	44	2	1	0
2009	41	31	0	9	1
2010	37	31	0	6	0
2011	29	26	1	2	0
2012	41	37	0	4	0
2013	51	46	0	4	1
2014	48	35	1	12	0
2015	37	30	1	4	1
2016	31	32	0	1	1
2017	37	29	0	6	2
2018	69	49	3	10	7
2019	73	62	0	6	5
2020	57	50	0	4	3
2021	64	40	0	8	16
2022	88	62	2	13	11

Source: German Ministry of the Interior (various years).

Table 6.4   Antisemitic Crimes by Perpetrator in Germany (2002–2022)

Year	Antisemitic Crimes	Right-Wing	Left-Wing	Foreign Ideology	Other
2002	1771	1594	6	89	82
2003	1344	1226	6	53	59
2004	1449	1346	4	46	53
2005	1748	1682	7	33	26
2006	1809	1662	4	89	54
2007	1657	1561	1	59	36
2008	1559	1496	5	41	17
2009	1690	1520	4	101	65
2010	1268	1192	1	53	22
2011	1239	1188	6	24	21
2012	1374	1314	3	38	19
2013	1275	1218	0	31	26
2014	1596	1342	7	176	71
2015	1366	1246	5	78	37
2016	1468	1381	2	48	37
2017	1504	1412	1	71	20
2018	1799	1603	14	102	80
2019	2032	1898	6	57	71
2020	2351	2224	10	40	77
2021	3027	2552	6	127	342
2022	2641	2185	8	67	381

Source: German Ministry of the Interior (various years).

why the primary focus of efforts to reduce antisemitism remain on the far-right, considering those adhering to such ideologies tend to commit the vast majority of violent antisemitic attacks and crimes. However, these efforts have been demonstrably less successful in recent years with sharp increases in such violence since 2018.

The data in Table 6.4 reflect similar trends to those in Table 6.3, in that both show that right-wing ideology tends to be the predominant ideology of perpetrators of antisemitic crime. Right-wing perpetrators commit 83 percent of violent antisemitic attacks, and an even higher percentage of total antisemitic crimes at 91 percent. The data nonetheless show that from 2010 to 2013, the number of antisemitic crimes tended to be lower than in previous years for most categories of perpetrator, including those of right-wing ideology. The year 2014, however, stands out as a five-year high point in antisemitic crimes, and perhaps most notable is the sharp increase in crimes committed by perpetrators of foreign ideologies. Antisemitic crimes committed by those of foreign ideology increased more than 500 percent from 31 in 2013 to 176 in 2014. One can cite numerous potential explanations for this increase; however, most plausible is perhaps the role of the Israel-Gaza conflict in the summer of that year in stoking manifestations of antisemitism. So, while opposition to Israeli policy itself may not be considered anti-semitism, controversy surrounding the State of Israel can indeed play into antisemitic narratives resulting in violence or crime against even non-Israeli Jews.

The data in this section show that antisemitic violent attacks and crimes in Germany have not followed linear trends and suggest that the strategies aimed to counter antisemitism have had mixed results. While the number of attacks and crimes tended to increase until 2007, those numbers generally declined until 2018, at which point they began reaching new highs. Of course, there are other variables that may also account for these trends, such as size of the domestic Jewish population and external events. Although right-wing ideologies tend to be responsible for a vast majority of antisemitic incidents in Germany, the data for perpetrators of what are classified as foreign ideologies tend to be especially volatile in particular years. German strategies for countering antisemitism have shown some success in terms of decreasing general antisemitic attitudes, but this has not necessarily been reflected in the crime data. A possible explanation for this is that while existing strategies may be successful in driving some away from antisemitic ideologies, they have been less successful with regard to influencing those individuals motivated enough to commit acts of violence or other crimes. Monitoring these trends further into the future will naturally provide more insight into the strategy effectiveness long-term.

Jewish Perceptions and Revival

To better understand the situation for Jewish communities in Germany, it is important not only to look at the raw numbers of antisemitic groups, attitudes, and incidents, but also to consider the perceptions and vibrancy of the domestic Jewish population. A fundamental aspect of many of the German policies to counter antisemitism has been to in essence rebuild much of the Jewish life in the country that had been lost to the Holocaust and persecution of Jews more generally. As explained in previous chapters, this has been attempted through various means, such as encouraging Jewish immigration, engaging Jewish groups and other NGOs, and providing funding and other support to cultural and even some religious institutions. Yet despite these efforts, many German Jews continue to perceive antisemitism as an increasing problem in Germany.

The European Union Agency for Fundamental Rights (FRA) took surveys in 2012 and 2018 to monitor the experiences and perceptions of antisemitism from the perspectives of European Jews. In 2012, 62 percent of German Jews responded that antisemitism is either a "very big" or a "fairly big" problem in the country, and that percentage increased to 85 percent in 2018. Similarly, in 2012 68 percent of German Jews responded that "the level of antisemitism has increased a lot or increased a little over the past 5 years" and this percentage increased to 89 percent in 2018. Furthermore, in 2018 41 percent of German Jews reported having experienced antisemitic harassment in the previous year, and 52 percent reported experiencing such harassment in the previous five years. Of those harassed, only 20 percent reported their most serious incident to police or another organization (EU Agency for Fundamental Rights, 2018). It is worth noting that in the years prior to 2018 levels of antisemitic attitudes, crimes, and violent attacks in Germany appeared to be declining and were at levels substantially lower than in the following years. However, this apparent progress was not perceived as such by a majority of the domestic Jewish community. Also concerning as it pertains to the government's efforts is that in 2018 only 49 percent of German Jews responded that the government responds effectively to the security needs of Jewish communities, and only 22 percent responded that the government combats antisemitism effectively (EU Agency for Fundamental Rights, 2018).

In terms of where German Jews have experienced antisemitic statements, the 2018 survey showed the Internet to be most prevalent, with 82 percent reporting they had experienced such statements in the previous year. The Internet was followed by social situations (56 percent), public spaces (53 percent), political events (52 percent), media other than the Internet (50 percent), political speeches or discussions (35 percent), and academia (29 percent) as the most frequent forums where antisemitic statements have been experienced (EU Agency for Fundamental Rights, 2018). As was mentioned in previous chapters, the Internet is a difficult forum to regulate and an area where efforts to counter antisemitism have not been well developed. Furthermore, issues of jurisdiction make it extremely difficult to enforce existing laws regarding antisemitic and other hate speech in such forums. Therefore, it is unsurprising that the

Internet has become the primary means by which antisemitic statements have tended to spread.

Despite these negative experiences and perceptions among German Jews, there have nonetheless been some indications of a Jewish revival in the country. In the period from 1990 to 2014, Germany had become home to the world's fastest-growing Jewish population (Associated Press, 2014). This is in part due to the country's loosening of immigration law for Jewish immigrants—90 percent of German Jews are, in fact, immigrants (Ben-Rafael, 2015: 57). In 1990, there were fewer than 30,000 Jews in Germany, but by 2012 there were over 100,000 who belonged to Jewish religious communities. Included in these increases are some 20,000 Israeli Jews who immigrated to Germany (Crossland, 2012). These increases resulted in Germany becoming not only the fastest-growing, but also the third-largest Jewish population in Europe following France and the United Kingdom (Ben-Rafael, 2015: 59). Although Jewish immigration to Germany has slowed since 2015, estimates in 2023 placed the core Jewish population in the country (meaning those who self-identify as Jewish) at approximately 118,000 with some wider estimates of the enlarged Jewish population at 225,000 (Institute for Jewish Policy Research, 2023).

With the increases in Germany's Jewish population, the number of Jewish institutions and representations of the religion have also been on the rise within a number of German cities. From 1990 to 2018, the number of synagogues in Germany increased from only a handful to 130 (Deutsche Welle, 2018). While this number is still far less than the 2,800 synagogues that were in the country in 1933, there has nonetheless been a notable increase since German reunification. Cities, such as Mainz, Dresden, Essen, and others, whose synagogues were either destroyed or heavily damaged by the Nazis or fighting in World War II have only since 2000 had these structures rebuilt (Deutsche Welle, 2018).

One city that perhaps best represents the revival of Jewish life in contemporary Germany is the eastern German city of Leipzig. Leipzig historically had one of the most active Jewish populations on German lands since at least the thirteenth century, as it served as a central location for Jewish traders throughout Europe. In 1935, Leipzig's Jewish community consisted of some 11,500 members, making it the sixth-largest Jewish community in Germany at the time. But by February 1945, all Jews in the city had either emigrated or were killed or deported. In the following decades, Leipzig's Jewish community was virtually nonexistent, with a total of only 35 reported members in 1991 (Virtual Jewish Library, 2023). However, largely through increased immigration, the city's Jewish community increased to some 1,300 members by 2019 (Deutsche Welle, 2019). The role of Jewish immigration in the city was exemplified in 2010 when two rabbis, originally from Lithuania and Uzbekistan, were ordained at a ceremony attended by more than 300 German and foreign Jewish leaders (Deutsche Welle, 2010). To better serve the growing Jewish community in the city, Leipzig's first kosher restaurant since the 1930s, Café Salomon, opened in 2019 (Deutsche Welle, 2019). Although it is only one case, the developments in Leipzig demonstrate how German policy reforms have helped facilitate the regrowth of Jewish communities that had been lost for decades.

As Jewish communities have grown throughout the country, both Jewish organizations and even the German government have placed an emphasis on bolstering the country's theology schools to train a greater number of rabbis domestically. In 2013, on the seventy-fifth anniversary of *Kristallnacht*, the University of Potsdam opened the first state-funded Jewish theology school in Europe. At the school's opening, German president Joachim Gauck stated, "In Germany, of all places, where the Jewish intelligentsia . . . was expelled and murdered, Jewish theology is finally being given its proper role" (Ferber, 2014). The theology school opened with fifty students and six newly appointed professors focusing on the subjects of Jewish liturgy and history. An important motivation behind opening the school has been to help put Judaism in Germany on equal footing with Christianity and Islam in order to both help revive the religion within the country and create new opportunities for interfaith dialogue (Ferber, 2014). In addition to the opening of new synagogues, the opening of new Jewish cultural institutions, and an increasing Jewish population, the country's first modern school of Jewish theology is an important marker in the country's wider Jewish revival.

Conclusion

The data from the German case indicate that the country's approach to combating antisemitism has had greater effectiveness in some areas than others. Many of the German legal and public diplomacy measures have specifically targeted far-right groups, in large part due to the fact that such groups commit an overwhelming majority of antisemitic crimes and violent attacks. The data indicate that this approach has shown some effectiveness in terms of reducing far-right group membership, as membership in such groups fell approximately two-thirds from the early 1990s to 2014. However, these groups have recouped some of that loss in the years since with an 81 percent increase in membership from 2014 to 2022. There has also been a substantial shift in the political support for far-right parties. Prior to 2014, the two main far-right parties, the NPD and Die Republikaner, obtained less than 2.5 percent of the votes cast in Bundestag elections since reunification. However, the rise of the AfD since 2014 has allowed far-right politics to become more mainstream and electorally successful at both the state and national levels. So, while Germany had appeared to be reducing the membership and influence of far-right groups and political parties from reunification until 2014, the period since has reversed those trends and has raised new questions as to how the country's approach should adjust to these challenges.

On the other hand, survey data indicate that general antisemitic attitudes have consistently fallen in Germany since 2002. The data indicate that strategies to counter antisemitism have been relatively effective in terms of decreasing general antisemitic attitudes within the country. Nonetheless, whereas antisemitic attitudes have declined over time, xenophobic attitudes have tended to be more prevalent, especially in eastern Germany. These data are important considering that 90 percent of German Jews are immigrants. Therefore, members of Germany's Jewish community may potentially face hostility for either reason, or the precise motivation of perpetrators in such cases may not always be decipherable. Thus, while general antisemitic attitudes may have decreased in the country since 2002, the prevalence of xenophobic attitudes also poses a threat to the domestic Jewish community's well-being.

Antisemitic crimes and violent attacks generally increased in Germany from 1991 to 2007 but then largely decreased until 2017. However, since 2018 such crimes and violent attacks have sharply increased to new highs. There are a few possible explanations for these trends. First, large increases in Germany's Jewish population led to more antisemitic attacks and crimes, in part because there were simply more Jews who could potentially become targeted for such acts. Second, external events may at times stoke antisemitic attitudes and behavior, thus leading to a higher number of attacks and crimes. And third, the approaches to countering antisemitism in the country may be slow to adapt to political and social change.

Despite arguable successes in some areas, such as reducing general antisemitic attitudes, German Jews have since at least 2012 perceived antisemitism to be an increasing problem within the country. And in 2018, approximately half said they had experienced some form of antisemitic harassment in the previous five years—with only 20 percent of those having reported such incidents to authorities. Nonetheless, Germany has since 1990 had one of the world's fastest-growing Jewish populations—having more than tripled by 2012. Consequently, the country has shown signs of a Jewish revival since reunification with increases in not only population, but also the number of Jewish religious, cultural, and educational institutions. These factors indicate that while many German Jews report antisemitism as an increasing problem, Germany also remains an attractive destination for many Jews worldwide.

7

Evaluating
Poland's Efforts

IN THIS CHAPTER, I EMPIRICALLY EVALUATE THE EFFECTIVENESS OF
Poland's strategies to combat antisemitism. The data analyzed include
support for far-right parties and groups, levels of antisemitic attitudes
and hate crimes, and the perceptions and vibrancy of the domestic Jewish community, and as with the previous chapter, the data afford a better understanding of the areas where these strategies have been most
and least effective. Particularly important to note is whether there have
been changes in the data after a policy was adopted. As explained in
Chapter 5, the first policies implemented were the legal measures introduced with the adoption of the country's constitution and penal code in
1997. The public diplomacy initiatives in Poland were implemented in
two parts. First, Poland focused on correcting mischaracterizations of
the country's history with the adoption of the Framework Program in
2002. Later, these efforts were expanded and began to include a more
direct emphasis on domestic engagement beginning in 2005. This timeline of policy implementation will be important with regard to the data
analysis in this chapter.

The Influence of Far-Right Groups

As mentioned in the previous chapter, German strategies toward antisemitism have shown some effectiveness with regard to decreasing the
membership and influence of far-right groups in the country over
time. In Poland, the strategies developed to counter antisemitism have

been less focused on such groups. Although Poland does monitor hate crimes in the country, the Polish government does not track membership statistics for far-right groups nor for antisemitic groups. This makes it difficult to directly compare the size and influence of such groups in these two countries over time. Nonetheless, one area where a more direct comparison can be made is in the realm of electoral politics. While Poland does not have reliable statistics for total far-right and antisemitic group membership, election results in the country provide some indications of the influence and support for groups with such ideology.

Poland has a few parties that promote an overtly antisemitic ideology, including the National Rebirth of Poland (NOP; registered in 1992), National Radical Camp (ONR; registered in 1993), and the Polish National Party (PNP; registered in 2004, deregistered in 2014). These parties, while known for their media campaigns, have not consistently run candidates for either parliamentary or regional elections. In fact, none of these parties has received above 0.3 percent of the national vote in any parliamentary election since their founding—far short of the 5 percent threshold needed to attain representation in the Sejm or Senat. The most electorally successful year for antisemitic parties in Poland was 2005, in which the PNP received 34,127 total votes (0.29 percent) and the NOP received 7,376 total votes (0.06 percent). However, none of these parties have appeared on national parliamentary ballots since 2011 (National Electoral Commission of Poland, 2023).

These data suggest that parties with an overtly antisemitic ideology tend to be less successful in Polish electoral politics than similar parties in Germany, such as the NPD and Die Republikaner. Nonetheless, there are segments in other, more successful nationalist parties that have expressed antisemitic views, although these views are not necessarily embraced by the party as a whole. This is particularly the case with more nationalistic parties, which often subscribe to a Catholic nationalist ideology. For example, former Polish defense minister and deputy leader of the Law and Justice party, Antoni Macierewicz, has expressed his belief that the Jewish conspiracy laid out in *The Protocols of the Elders of Zion* could be real. Macierewicz told a listener during a 2002 Radio Maryja interview that "experience shows that there are such groups in Jewish circles" when asked about the conspiracy (Syal, 2015). Another member of Law and Justice, Senator Dorota Arciszewska-Mielewczyk, controversially suggested that Polish Jews are represented by the Knesset and not the Polish parliament in January 2014 in response to a report on antisemitism that was delivered to the Polish parliament (Coordination Forum for Countering Antisemitism, 2014). These statements demonstrate that while overtly antisemitic parties in Poland may not achieve widespread electoral success, there are indeed elements within, particularly nationalist parties, that have expressed antisemitic beliefs.

Antisemitic rhetoric became front and center during the 2020 presidential campaign, particularly regarding the issue of restitution payments for Jews who lost property during World War II. The Law and Justice candidate, and incumbent Polish president, Andrzej Duda accused that his opponent, Warsaw mayor Rafał Trzaskowski, "will fulfill Jewish demands" in response to Trzaskowski saying "of course we have to talk to Jewish groups and try to resolve this" (Cienski, 2020). Echoing Duda's criticism, Law and Justice leader Jarosław Kaczyński said of Trzaskowski, "Only someone without a Polish soul, a Polish heart and a Polish mind could say something like that. Mr. Trzaskowski doesn't have them, seeing as he says that this is open for discussion" (Cienski, 2020). In response to the narrative that Trzaskowski would "fulfill Jewish demands," Poland's chief rabbi Michael Schudrich observed that "the Jewish community of Poland was shocked that President Duda made a statement that specifically appealed to the votes of antisemites" (Lazaroff, 2020). So, while Law and Justice may not run on an overtly antisemitic platform in the manner of some other Polish political parties, some of its candidates for office have employed antisemitic rhetoric to appeal to voters. In a similar manner to Germany's AfD, Law and Justice have appealed to Poland's far-right voters while also being considered by many to be mainstream. This has allowed the party to achieve electoral success serving in a coalition government from 2005 to 2007 and later becoming the ruling party in 2015 and holding its plurality with 43.6 percent of the vote in the 2019 parliamentary elections (National Electoral Commission of Poland, 2023).

Beyond the electoral results, the lack of reliable data on far-right and other antisemitic groups in Poland makes it difficult to fully evaluate the extent that efforts to counter antisemitism have had on such groups over time. Overtly antisemitic groups that have been organized and registered as political parties tend to be rather minor and have not achieved significant success in modern elections. However, this does not necessarily mean that general antisemitic attitudes are at a lower level in Poland, only that antisemitic ideology has not been particularly influential as an organized, distinct movement in contemporary Polish politics. Those leaders who have expressed antisemitic beliefs have tended to be within nationalist elements of other major parties that do not necessarily have antisemitism as a core tenet of their platform, thus making them more difficult to identify as a distinct, organized group. This lack of clearly defined, popular antisemitic and far-right groups in Poland makes it more difficult to target policies toward such groups, as is often done in the German case. In order to achieve a better understanding of the results in Poland, it may be more beneficial to examine more general survey data on antisemitic attitudes, which tend to be more frequently collected and reliable.

Antisemitic Attitudes

The data most consistently collected in Poland with regard to antisemitism since the end of communist rule have been attitude surveys. Since 1993, the Public Opinion Research Center based in Warsaw has collected annual survey data on the sympathy and antipathy among Poles toward Jews. These data are displayed in Figure 7.1.

As the data show, sympathy toward Jews was lowest among Poles in the first year for which data was collected (Public Opinion Research Center, 1993) at only 15 percent, while antipathy was also at its highest

Figure 7.1   Sympathy and Antipathy Toward Jews in Poland (1993–2022)

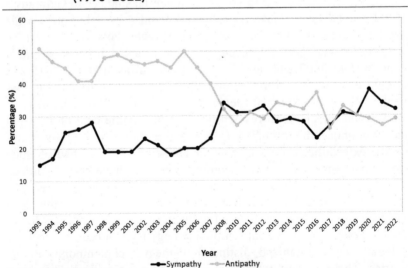

Source: Public Opinion Research Center (various years).

level in the same year at over 50 percent. With a few exceptions, the data remained relatively consistent until about 2005 when sympathy began to increase and antipathy began to decrease. This change is especially notable, because this is the time period in which many of Poland's strategies to counter antisemitism had become fully implemented. As noted in previous chapters, Poland's legal response to antisemitism began in 1997 with the adoption of the country's constitution and penal codes, both of which include punishments for hate crimes against Jews and other groups based on nationality, ethnicity, race, or religion. However, there was little to no immediate impact on Polish attitudes toward Jews in the years following the adoption and implementation of these laws. In fact, attitudes toward Jews tended to become more negative in the years following 1997 (sympathy dropped from 28 percent to 19 percent in 1998). One possible explanation for this is that the legal measures were more intended to prevent acts of violence against Jews than to influence attitudes specifically. These legal measures were largely intended to provide a deterrent to those who may commit acts of violence or promote hateful speech and less to change the attitudes of those who may not act violently yet have antipathy toward Jews.

Another aspect of Poland's legal approach was the establishment of the Institute of National Remembrance (IPN), which was founded in 1998 and began operation in 2000 (Institute of National Remembrance, 2023c). It is important to remember that the IPN is not merely limited to prosecuting crimes relating to Nazism and communism, but also is involved in determining the facts with regard to Nazi and communist crimes, such as the Holocaust. These latter tasks are carried out through the Bureau of Provision and Archivization of Documents. So, while the IPN is indeed a part of Poland's legal response to antisemitism, it also engages in debates and corrects misinformation about a number of groups, including Jews, and the crimes committed against them. In this way, one may consider the IPN as an organization that straddles the lines between the legal and public diplomacy approaches, as the organization is engaged in both the prosecution of hate crimes and influencing public opinion and knowledge. As the data show, the IPN did not have an immediate effect on Polish attitudes toward Jews in the five years following its establishment in 2000. However, the sorts of historical research and educational goals of the organization are likely to take time to develop, so one may expect these measures not to have immediate impacts on public opinion. It is nonetheless possible that such measures have made an impact in the long-term.

The most noticeable declines in antipathy and increases in sympathy toward Jews began after 2005. While it is true that Poland's public diplomacy campaign had its roots in 2002 with the establishment of the Framework Program, these early initiatives were primarily concerned with correcting mischaracterizations abroad in order to gain support for Polish accession to the European Union. It was not until 2005, after Poland had achieved EU accession, that the public diplomacy initiatives became more internally focused. This internal focus included the promotion of Jewish cultural events, educational initiatives, dialogical forums, and greater outreach to Jewish communities. It is indeed noteworthy that the most pronounced shift with regard to positive attitudes toward Jews began shortly after the implementation of such programs. In 2005, approximately 50 percent of Poles had antipathy toward Jews, but by 2010 this number was reduced by nearly half to 27 percent. It is also worth noting that 2008 was the first time recorded in which Poles had more sympathy toward Jews than antipathy. Since that time, levels of sympathy and antipathy have been relatively even, whereas in most years prior to the public diplomacy campaign the levels of antipathy toward Jews were nearly twice the levels of sympathy. This chronology suggests that the implementation of a domestically focused public diplomacy campaign led to more positive attitudes among Poles toward Jews.

These assertions are reflected in other survey research covering the same period as well. In 2002, before the public diplomacy components focusing on domestic factors were fully implemented, 20 percent of Polish respondents believed that Jews were responsible for conspiring to negatively influence Polish politics. That figure was reduced to only 6 percent by 2011 (Borger and Vasagar, 2011). In 2002, 43 percent of Polish respondents said that Jews have too much influence within Polish society; that number was decreased to 22 percent by 2010 (Sulek, 2012). Perhaps most encouraging for the future of Poland's domestic environment and a reason why levels of antipathy toward Jews have decreased, survey data from 2008 showed that levels of antisemitism among Polish youth were quite low. According to Ireneusz Krzemiński's scale of modern antisemitism, only 5 percent of seventeen to eighteen-year-old Polish students held strongly antisemitic beliefs, whereas 27 percent of Polish adults held such beliefs (Ambrosewicz-Jacobs, 2013).

Although sympathetic attitudes toward Jews have generally increased in Poland since the 1990s, recent data have shown increases in particular manifestations of antisemitism, particularly religious and economic antisemitism. Figures 7.2 and 7.3 show survey data from 2009, 2013, and 2017 regarding two of the most common beliefs in religious antisemitism—Jewish responsibility for the death of Jesus Christ and accusations of blood libel.

Figure 7.2 Jews Are Responsible for the Death of Jesus Christ (Polish Opinion)

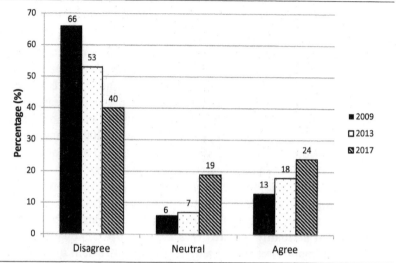

Source: Center for Research on Prejudice (2023).

Figure 7.3 Jews Use Christian Blood for Ritual Purposes (Polish Opinion)

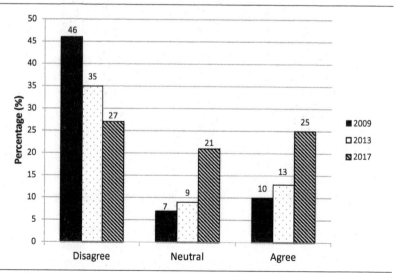

Source: Center for Research on Prejudice (2023).

While many Poles disagree with the statement that Jews are responsible for the death of Jesus Christ, the data show that the antisemitic belief in deicide increased over time. Whereas 66 percent disagreed with the claims in 2009, only 53 percent disagreed in 2013, and that percentage decreased even further to 40 percent in 2017. And whereas only 13 percent believed such claims in 2009, that number increased to 18 percent in 2013 and 24 percent in 2017. These data do not necessarily contradict the data in Figure 7.1 but do show that religious antisemitism has become more prevalent as a manifestation over the years measured.

Figure 7.3 demonstrates that belief in blood libel also increased from 2009 to 2017. Whereas 46 percent of Poles in 2009 disagreed with the claim that Jews use Christian blood for ritual purposes, only 35 percent disagreed with such a statement in 2013, and that percentage decreased further to 27 percent in 2017. The percentage who agreed increased from 10 percent in 2009 to 13 percent in 2013 and 25 percent in 2017. These data indicate that although general attitudes regarding sympathy and antipathy toward Jews have improved since the 1990s, there are still manifestations of antisemitism that remain prevalent and have even increased in recent years. The periods measured in Figures 7.2 and 7.3 are after the most prominent legal and public diplomacy measures combating antisemitism were implemented, so these data suggest that the strategies were not particularly effective in reducing certain manifestations of antisemitism, in this case religious antisemitism. While the legal measures implemented in the 1990s do provide punishments for antisemitic behavior, these measures are not necessarily designed to directly influence attitudes. Influencing attitudes is more in the domain of the public diplomacy responses, which have shown some effectiveness in terms of reducing antipathy toward Jews but have not necessarily been as effective in reducing the prevalence of certain religiously antisemitic myths.

Another manifestation of antisemitism that has long existed in Poland, as it has elsewhere, is economic antisemitism. As explained in earlier chapters, ever since their arrival in Poland in the tenth century, Jews have played an integral role in the development of the Polish economy. Educated Jews from neighboring lands who faced persecution were often invited by Polish kings for their expertise in obtaining capital and financial resources to develop industry and agriculture. However, the relative success of many Jews in the Polish economy contributed to a feeling of grievance and resentment among some Poles. These grievances were exploited throughout history, especially during the early twentieth century by the National Democrats, the Nazis during their occupation of

Poland, and the postwar communist government led by the Soviet Union. Jews had often been cited as a scapegoat to deflect attention from each of these regimes' numerous failures. This deep-rooted history of economic antisemitism perpetuated for generations by various governments would seem difficult to counter.

One may assume that as Poland has improved its economy since the fall of communism in 1989, economically driven antisemitism would decline; however, the data in Figure 7.4 show that this does not seem to be the case. The percentage of Poles who agree with the statement that "Jews have too much economic influence" has generally increased from 1992 to 2023.

Of the years measured, 1992 had the lowest level of those asserting economically antisemitic attitudes at 36 percent. However, this percentage increased to 57 percent by 2014. One may expect that the economic hardships related to the shock therapy approach to maketization and liberalization of the Polish economy in the 1990s would have triggered more negative attitudes toward Jews in terms of their economic influence. As data before 1992 is unavailable, it is not possible to fully examine this hypothesis, but the data in Figure 7.4 do

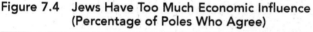

Figure 7.4 Jews Have Too Much Economic Influence (Percentage of Poles Who Agree)

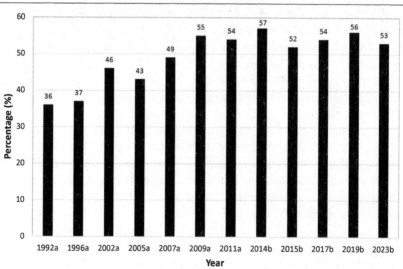

Source: a. Bilewicz (2012).
b. Anti-Defamation League (various years).

show that economic antisemitism did indeed increase in the 2000s—even after market liberalization was largely accomplished. It is also worth noting that the periods from 2005–2007 and 2007–2009 each experienced rather large 6 percent increases in economic antisemitism. From 2005–2007, the government was controlled by the more right-wing, national-conservative Law and Justice party, and from 2007–2009, the government was controlled by the more center-right Civic Platform. Therefore, these same 6 percent increases occurred regardless of government ideology. One may expect events such as the 2008 global economic recession to increase economic grievances, and although economic antisemitism did rise in the following years, such attitudes have generally increased over a nearly thirty-year period. Consequently, the data suggest that neither the legal nor public diplomacy responses to antisemitism have been particularly effective in reducing attitudes reflecting economic antisemitism.

The data in this section demonstrate that although general Polish sympathy toward Jews has increased since the end of the Cold War, levels of religious and economic antisemitism have not reflected such improvement—and, in fact, seem to have worsened. In terms of general Polish attitudes toward Jews, the changes reflecting more positive attitudes became most pronounced following the implementation of public diplomacy strategies in 2005. The implementation of legal policies in the 1990s seemed to have far less of an effect, which may in large part be due to the fact that such policies are more intended to prevent certain violent behaviors rather than alter perceptions and attitudes—a goal more closely associated with the public diplomacy strategy.

Perhaps one explanation as to why Poles have tended to have greater sympathy toward Jews over time, yet increasing levels of religious and economic antisemitism, is the messaging used in the public diplomacy campaigns. The primary emphasis of Poland's public diplomacy campaign has been to focus on common connections between Poles and Jews. This has been done via initiatives, such as promoting Jewish cultural events and institutions, dialogical forums, educational programs, and other similar measures. However, there has not been a similar emphasis on dispelling antisemitic myths, in particular those relating to religion and the economy. This focus within Poland's public diplomacy messaging may help to explain why Poles have over time developed more sympathetic attitudes toward Jews, yet an increasing number accept certain religious and economic myths. This discrepancy may expose one of the flaws in Poland's public diplomacy strategy and an area for future improvement.

Victimhood Competition

A unique aspect of antisemitism in Poland, which is related to the issue of Holocaust denial, is what is known as victimhood competition. Victimhood competition describes the argument between groups, often ethnic groups, over which group suffered worse during a particular period in history—in this case World War II and the Holocaust. Some Poles tend to view sympathy regarding the Holocaust as a zero-sum game—either Poles suffered or Jews, but not both. This controversy has become increasingly prominent since 1989 when activists began placing crosses at Auschwitz-Birkenau. By 1998, there were over 240 crosses placed at the site. Proponents of the cross placement argued that the crosses were meant to honor the 100,000 Poles killed at the camp, while critics argued that the crosses were intended to discount the more than 1 million Jews killed there (Zubrzycki, 2006).

The example of the crosses at Auschwitz-Birkenau is emblematic of the larger issue of victimhood competition in Poland that many psychologists argue spurs ethnic conflict and animosity. Many argue that competitive victimhood reduces trust and empathy toward out-group members (Noor, Brown, and Prentice, 2008). Michał Bilewicz of the University of Warsaw found that Poles who consider their nation an eternal victim of aggression from foreign powers tended to possess antisemitic attitudes more often. Bilewicz also found that those who perceived Poles to be more victimized in the past than Jews had significantly more anti-Jewish attitudes (Bilewicz, 2012: 2813).

Notably, this issue of victimhood competition appears to have been increasing in Poland over time. Data show that the number of Poles who acknowledge Jews as the most numerous victims of the wartime period in Poland has decreased since 1992. In 1992, 46 percent of Poles agreed that Jews were the most numerous victims of World War II and the Holocaust in Poland; in 2002, this was 38 percent; and by 2010, only 28 percent agreed. Over the same period, the number of Poles who think that ethnic Poles were the most numerous victims of World War II and the Holocaust has increased. In 1992, only 6 percent agreed with this claim; in 2002, this increased to 9 percent; and in 2010, it was up to 15 percent (Bilewicz, 2012: 2813). Bilewicz attributes these numbers to two things. First, the generation of people who remember the Nazi occupation of Poland has been disappearing from Polish society. More than seventy years removed from the Holocaust and World War II, many who directly experienced the period are no longer available to provide firsthand accounts. Second, Holocaust education in the country has not been particularly effective in conveying the extent of destruction to the Jewish community and dispelling myths (Bilewicz, 2012: 2813).

These trends are particularly worrisome among Polish youth, a substantial portion of whom tend to believe that Jews exploit the Holocaust for their own purposes. Survey results from 2012 showed that 30 percent of Polish youth believed that Jews abuse Polish feelings of guilt and more than 40 percent believed that Jews would like to receive compensation from Poland for the Nazi atrocities (Bilewicz, 2012: 2813). These accusations tend to align with historical antisemitic fears of Jews exploiting the Polish people. An important aspect of postwar antisemitism to remember is that not only Holocaust denial, but also specific evaluations of the Holocaust may be used as a tool to communicate antisemitic beliefs or attitudes. Survey results have shown that there is a portion of Poles who appreciate the fact that the Holocaust ended the thousand-year existence of a large-scale Jewish community in Poland. In a 2010 study, 19.6 percent of Poles surveyed agreed with the following statement: "Although the Holocaust was a great tragedy, one good thing about it is that there are no more Jews living currently in Poland" (Kucia, 2010). These results demonstrate that while general sympathy among Poles toward Jews has increased since the early 1990s, there are areas of postwar antisemitism, and particularly as it relates to victimhood competition, that have increased. These results are particularly notable among Polish youth and show that there is significant room for improvement regarding Poland's Holocaust education efforts.

Antisemitic Crimes

The legal measures intended to quell antisemitic behavior and hate crimes in Poland have largely been in place since 1997 with the adoption of the country's modern constitution and penal code. These laws were established with the intent to punish hate speech, incitement, and violence against groups on the basis of religion, ethnicity, nationality, or race. The laws have been in place for over two decades, but there has not yet been a study evaluating their actual effects on antisemitic hate crimes within the country. Perhaps one reason for this is that Poland has lacked credible reporting mechanisms regarding hate crimes, and those datasets that exist do not tend to show consistent trends. Prior to 2015, the Human Rights Protection Team within the Ministry of the Interior was tasked with collecting data and reporting on antisemitic incidents; however, the data collected by the team was through communications with human rights and minority community organizations rather than official government sources and was only published from 2010 to 2014. The datasets were also unclear in terms of what acts were considered antisemitic incidents. Nonetheless, Figure 7.5 shows the data collected during those years.

The data in Figure 7.5 show that antisemitic incidents in Poland decreased from 30 in 2010 to 21 in 2012, but then increased to 39 by 2014. The data collected for these five years do not show any clear trend, perhaps in part due to the relatively short time interval over which the data was collected. Nonetheless, these data show a similar increase in antisemitic incidents in 2014 to that in Germany. Once again, a likely explanation for this sharp increase is external events, in particular the Israel-Gaza War, which took place in the summer of that year. These data, however, were not collected consistently nor in a systematic way, thus limiting their utility.

Since 2016, Poland's Ministry of the Interior and the country's police have developed a shared hate crime data collection system, which is intended to provide more accurate data than the earlier efforts by the Human Rights Protection Team. While there are no general guidelines for hate crime recording, Polish police officers are required

Figure 7.5   Antisemitic Crimes Reported in Poland (2010–2014)

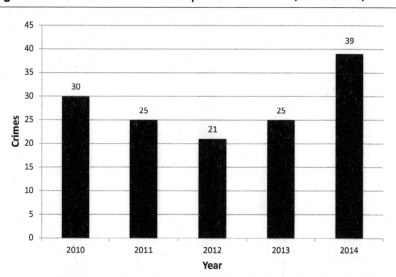

Source: EU Agency for Fundamental Rights (2015).

to establish whether a perpetrator was acting on a biased motivation, and this is noted on both the incident forms and police force's electronic database (OSCE, 2023b). Figure 7.6 graphs the number of total antisemitic crimes reported by Polish police from 2016 to 2021.

The data from 2016 to 2021 do not indicate a consistent trend, although most years show significantly more antisemitic crimes than in Figure 7.5. However, this may in large part be due to the different manner in which data was collected. It is therefore not possible to accurately compare the data in Figures 7.5 and 7.6. Nonetheless, it is likely that the higher numbers in more recent years are due to more systematic recording and reporting of such crime, which will consequently allow for increasingly accurate assessments in the future with a larger sample size.

The lack of consistently reported data regarding antisemitic hate crimes in Poland makes it difficult to make a clear determination as to the effectiveness of the efforts to counter antisemitism. However, it is noteworthy that the quantity of antisemitic crimes reported in Poland is far lower than in Germany during the years measured. For comparison, 2018 was the year in which Poland reported its highest number of antisemitic hate crimes with 197, whereas Germany in the same year totaled 1,799. The gap is even more drastic for 2020, where Poland totaled only 13 antisemitic crimes and Germany totaled 2,351.

Figure 7.6   Antisemitic Crimes Reported by Polish Police (2016–2021)

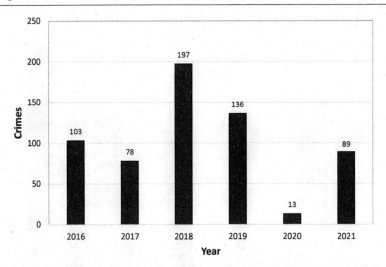

Source: OSCE (2023a).

There are three likely explanations for this difference in the quantity of antisemitic crimes. First, Poland has a much smaller Jewish population than Germany. Poland has an estimated Jewish population of between 3,200 and 10,000, whereas Germany has over 100,000 people who belong to Jewish religious communities and an estimated population of over 200,000 who have a Jewish background (Jewish Virtual Library, 2023; Yivo Institute for Jewish Research, 2023a; Crossland, 2012). Consequently, there are simply more Jews in Germany who may be targeted for antisemitic crimes. Second, definitions of what constitutes an antisemitic attack and the ways that data are collected may differ. Definitions of antisemitic attacks are indeed subjective and dependent upon the agency or individuals collecting such data. It is possible that officials in Poland may be more hesitant to label incidents as antisemitic than their counterparts in Germany. Third, it is also possible that the Polish efforts to counter antisemitism have been more effective in deterring crimes than those in Germany. This last explanation is more difficult to substantiate because Poland did not track data as far back in time or as consistently as Germany, and thus it is more difficult to determine the likely effects on antisemitic hate crimes. Nonetheless, at least since 2010, Poland has reported a far lower number of total antisemitic crimes. Each of these explanations may contribute to the vast differences in the total number of antisemitic crimes reported in each country.

Jewish Perceptions and Revival

As in the German case, it is important to look beyond the indicators already mentioned and also consider the perceptions and vibrancy of the domestic Jewish community. Much of Poland's public diplomacy strategy has been focused on incorporating Jewish history and culture into Polish identity. While Poland had Europe's largest Jewish community prior to World War II, Poland has not emphasized rebuilding that domestic community through migration to the extent that Germany has. Poland has instead emphasized the historic importance of Jews in its national history despite the near absence of a Jewish community in recent decades. Nonetheless, of those Jews who remain in Poland, many perceive antisemitism as an increasing problem in the country.

In their 2018 survey on the Jewish community's experiences and perceptions of antisemitism, the European Union's FRA found that 85 percent of Polish Jews considered antisemitism to be either a "very big" or "fairly big" problem within the country. The 2018 survey also found that 83 percent of Polish Jews responded that "the level of anti-semitism has increased a lot or increased a little over the past 5 years." Furthermore, 32 percent of Polish Jews reported experiencing antisemitic harassment in the past year, and 45 percent in the past five years. Of those who experienced harassment in the past five years, only 19 percent claimed to have reported their most serious incident to the police or another organization. Particularly concerning in terms of the government's efforts is that 22 percent of Polish Jews responded that they think the Polish government adequately responds to the security needs of Jewish communities, and only 7 percent think the government combats antisemitism effectively—the latter being the lowest percentage of the twelve EU countries surveyed (EU Agency for Fundamental Rights, 2018).

Similar to the German case, the Internet tends to be by far the forum in which Polish Jews are most likely to experience antisemitic statements. Of those Polish Jews who reported experiencing such statements, 92 percent reported doing so online. The Internet was followed by political events (65 percent), media other than the Internet (64 percent), public spaces (62 percent), social situations (57 percent), political speeches or discussions (48 percent), and academia (18 percent) as the most frequent forums where antisemitic statements have been experienced. Notably, Jews in Poland tended to report higher levels of antisemitic statements at political events, speeches, and discussions than those in the other eleven EU countries surveyed (EU Agency for Fundamental Rights, 2018). This is perhaps one reason why only 7 percent of Polish Jews think the government combats antisemitism effectively. Despite the efforts made by numerous agencies to address the problem, antisemitic political rhetoric concerning property restitution and other issues tends to undermine those efforts. The 92 percent of Polish Jews who reported experiencing antisemitic statements online is also the highest percentage of the twelve EU countries surveyed. However, no country reported a percentage lower than 77 percent, which suggests the proliferation of antisemitism online is a severe international problem with no coordinated strategy to counter it.

As has been the case in Germany, one of the measures taken by the Polish government to improve Polish-Jewish relations and demonstrate progress internationally has been to facilitate, and in some ways even promote, the revival of Judaism within the country. But unlike in the German case, Poland's efforts on this issue have not necessarily had increasing the domestic Jewish population as a goal. Instead its efforts have concentrated on rejecting the image of Poland representing a Jewish graveyard and further establishing credibility behind the message that Poland is a modern country that embraces, rather than discourages, diversity. The data above demonstrate there have certainly been challenges in terms of supporting that message. However, recent increases in Jewish cultural expression and institutions cannot be overlooked.

Estimates of Poland's Jewish population have ranged from 3,200 to 10,000 since the end of the Cold War (Jewish Virtual Library, 2023; Yivo Institute for Jewish Research, 2023a). Nonetheless, there has been an empirically verifiable increase in Jewish cultural events and organizations since 2000 specifically. The (re)opening of Jewish community centers and synagogues in major cities, the Krakow Jewish Culture Festival, the POLIN museum, and developments in the Kazimierz District and other areas all present evidence of some growth in terms of Jewish culture and civil society in contemporary Poland. Some may argue that Polish civil society as a whole has increased in recent years and the increase in Jewish institutions is simply a reflection of this phenomenon. This argument has some validity; however, the Jewish revival is unique due to the role of the Ministry of Foreign Affairs, other government agencies, and international NGOs. No other segment of Polish civil society has been nearly as much of an emphasis of public diplomacy efforts or experienced an increase in cultural activities, institutions, and influence so high compared to a group's proportion of the population.

These efforts have been notable in terms of returning Jewish culture to a prominent place within Poland's postcommunist identity, and, as I have argued, increases in Jewish populations do not tell the full story regarding Poland's Jewish revival. Nonetheless, the increased interest and prevalence of Jewish culture has led to notable increases in conversions to Judaism in recent years. Beit Warsaw, a Reformist Judaism congregation, began offering "Step-by-Step" conversion courses in 2003 and oversaw over 100 conversions by 2012 with another 80 enrollees with Jewish roots considering conversion at that time (Tzur, 2012). Other congregations have begun offering similar "Step-by-Step" courses that allow Poles to learn about Judaism with a possibility to convert (Beit Polska, 2023). According to Jewish leaders, conversion rates have increased in the twenty-first century, and as Krakow Jewish Community Center director Jonathan Ornstein describes, the increases in conversion to Judaism have been dubbed the "*Jewish* Jewish Revival." Ornstein goes on to state, "You are talking about a community that was frozen. It went underground. And now it's reemerging" and has added that "Thousands are walking around Poland with Jewish roots they still don't know they have" (Grollmus, 2012; Schwartz, 2019). Despite Poland's Jewish community having less than 10,000 registered members, Ornstein contends that there are up to 100,000 Poles with Jewish roots, many of whom are simply unaware of or do not understand the connection (Susskind, 2016). Many of those who have converted or are considering conversion are Poles who have discovered Jewish roots in their own families that their parents or grandparents may have masked during the Holocaust or communist rule. So although there have not yet been remarkable increases in Poland's total Jewish population, the increased prevalence of Jewish culture has the potential to lead to increases in conversions and consequently growth in the population and religiosity among Jewish believers.

Conclusion

The data from this chapter demonstrate that in some areas where the Polish government has placed the greatest emphasis in terms of healing Polish-Jewish relations, there have been positive results, in particular improving general Polish attitudes toward Jews. The general theme of Poland's public diplomacy campaign since 2005 has been to emphasize common connections between Poles and Jews—both historically and culturally. This has been done through cultural exchanges, holding dialogical forums, promoting Jewish cultural events, and emphasizing Jewish contributions to Polish society. The data in Figure 7.1 showed that since the implementation of this strategy, survey results of Poles have begun to reflect greater sympathy and less antipathy toward Jews. However, despite these improvements in general attitudes, other survey data has shown increases in religious and economic antisemitism within the country. This discrepancy indicates that while the focus on common connections between Poles and Jews may have made Poles more sympathetic toward Jews, the public diplomacy campaign has not necessarily been successful, or well-focused enough, with regard to dispelling antisemitic myths that have been perpetuated in the country for centuries. Thus, the public diplomacy campaign could be improved with more emphasis on such issues.

Another area where Poland's public diplomacy could be improved is in addressing the concept of victimhood competition. Survey data has shown since 1992 that greater percentages of Poles have been downplaying the effects of the Holocaust on the Jewish community. This may in part be due to inadequacies in the country's Holocaust education efforts. Also worrisome are survey data among the country's youth that show 30 percent believe Jews abuse feelings of Polish guilt. This concept of victimhood competition has not been specifically addressed in Poland's public diplomacy despite the fact that this has been an important aspect of postwar antisemitism in the country. From the available data, it is difficult to ascertain the effectiveness of Poland's policies with regard to antisemitic crimes committed in the country, as these data have not been collected reliably nor consistently over a long enough period. However, with the establishment of the Ministry of the Interior's shared hate crimes data collection system in 2016, there will likely be more available data to evaluate in the future.

Despite progress in some areas, an overwhelming majority of Polish Jews consider antisemitism to be an increasing problem in Polish society. Further, the domestic Jewish community is largely unsatisfied with the efforts by the government to counter the problem. A major reason for this is likely due to the fact that a majority of Polish Jews reported experiencing antisemitic statements at political events, speeches, and discussions. Nonetheless, as in the German case, Poland has simultaneously experienced a recent revival of Judaism within the country. However, the Jewish revival in Poland is less defined by increases in the actual Jewish population, but rather an increase in Jewish cultural expression and institutions. The revival can most clearly be seen in the increases in synagogues and Jewish community centers, cultural festivals, and Jewish-themed businesses. And although the revival is primarily defined by these cultural expressions and institutions, there has also been evidence of some Poles converting to Judaism due to factors such as increased interest in the religion's history in Poland and discoveries of Jewish roots within many families.

Taken together, the information in this chapter indicates that Poland's strategies toward antisemitism have made progress in some areas, such as increased sympathy among Poles toward Jews, as well as increases in Jewish cultural expression and institutions. Also revealed have been certain limitations to Poland's approach and potential areas for improvement, including providing a greater emphasis on dispelling antisemitic myths, addressing the issue of victimhood competition, and better responding to the experiences and perceptions of the domestic Jewish community. The following chapter will offer some final insights as to the connections between the German and Polish cases and areas where further investigation is needed.

8

The Path Forward

As I noted in Chapter 1, antisemitism is a term without a universally accepted definition. The definition that I have adopted in this book is "hostile attitudes or attacks targeting Jewish people, symbols, or interests based on religious, economic, racial, or political grounds." Antisemitism is most often measured using survey research assessing attitudes and crime data regarding attacks on Jewish people and property. Furthermore, the historical manifestations of antisemitism have developed from religious, economic, racial, and political hatred and grievances. The academic literature on the subject varies in terms of how many and which types of manifestations exist, but, as I have argued in the previous chapters, these four categories most accurately and concisely capture the historical development of the problem.

The historical development of antisemitism in both the German and Polish cases followed similar paths, with each country experiencing the four primary manifestations of antisemitism over time. In both cases, religious antisemitism preceded all other forms. Accusations of blood libel and deicide, along with other misunderstandings of Jewish religious practices, motivated many of the early persecutions of Jews in central Europe. Following the First Crusade, Jews in central Europe were often restricted to employment in socially inferior sectors such as moneylending and tax collection—in large part due to Christian prohibitions on usury. This development led to an often-adversarial relationship between Christian debtors and Jewish creditors that formed the basis for the next manifestation—economic antisemitism. Therefore, economic antisemitism was, in a way, borne out of religious antisemitism.

The depiction of greedy Jewish bankers among many Germans and Poles from the Middle Ages onward has often led to resentment and scapegoating for various societal ills. Such attitudes have been a continuing source of conspiracy theories, such as *The Protocols of the Elders of Zion*, and provided a common justification for Jewish persecution during times of economic turmoil.

In the nineteenth century, a combination of pseudoscientific theories, such as eugenics, and a rise in ethnic nationalism led to a new manifestation of antisemitism taking shape—racial antisemitism. At the core of racial antisemitism is the belief that one's Jewishness is not only determined by one's beliefs, but also one's blood. In many of the pseudoscientific theories of the time, the Jewish race was often considered inferior. After World War I, many Germans, in particular the Nazi Party, scapegoated Jews for their loss in the war and propagated ideas of an ideal, ethnically homogenous state—an ideal that did not include Jews. At the same time, many Catholic nationalists in the newly created independent Poland sought to establish a Catholic state—an ideal that also did not include Jews. These factors played a major role in sparking the violent antisemitism that led to expelling great numbers of Jews and eventually murdering millions in the Holocaust.

The fourth and most recent manifestation of antisemitism, also present in both countries, is political antisemitism. Political antisemitism includes numerous conspiracy theories, many relating to Zionist plots to undermine governments, as well as Holocaust denial and, particularly in Poland, the notion of victimhood competition. This manifestation often perpetuates theories that depict Jews as attempting to achieve gains by illegitimate or deceptive means, such as exaggerating, or even making up, the Holocaust to receive international sympathy for the Zionist movement or undermining governments through various means. These manifestations have centuries-long histories in both countries, have led to long periods of violence and persecution, and have become a problem that both the German and Polish governments have recently decided to address to help improve their respective countries' international reputation and standing.

In the post–Cold War period, both Germany and Poland have each had their own motivations to address the accusations and realities of historical and modern antisemitism. Each country has taken a similar approach in terms of implementing both legal and public diplomacy measures to counter the problem; however, the methods and chronology tend to differ in a few ways. In the German case, legal measures have included punishments for certain forms of hate speech, incitement, and Holocaust denial; easing immigration restrictions for Jews; and granting Judaism full legal status with certain protections. Germany's public diplomacy measures include assisting Jewish civil society organizations, promoting education initiatives for youth, and countering far-right group messaging and membership. Legal measures in Poland have included punishments for certain forms of hate speech, incitement, and Holocaust denial; establishing a central organization to investigate such crimes; allowing some Jews of Polish origin to return; and granting Judaism full legal status. Poland's public diplomacy has been primarily concerned with emphasizing a message demonstrating historical connections between Poles and Jews, providing support to Jewish cultural organizations, and correcting mischaracterizations regarding the Holocaust.

This book offers a unique theoretical finding with regard to public diplomacy—namely, the importance of *domestic engagement* when targeted to address an issue such as antisemitism. Much of the literature on public diplomacy focuses on the concept of "promotion" and a country's efforts to emphasize the positive aspects of its culture, political values, and foreign policies. However, events such as genocide can overwhelm international perceptions about a particular country and thus need to be addressed publicly. For international messaging on such issues to be credible, countries must first demonstrate domestic progress on these issues. This element of credibility is an important link between the domestic and international spheres. The cases of Germany and Poland and their public diplomacy efforts with regard to antisemitism are prime examples of this linkage.

The initiatives listed above provide the contours of each country's strategy to combat antisemitism. The strategies overlap in a number of ways: both countries have laws prohibiting certain antisemitic speech, incitement, and Holocaust denial; provide various means of support to domestic Jewish communities; and partner state and civil society organizations through public diplomacy initiatives. These strategies also differ in two major ways: whereas Germany has eased Jewish immigration restrictions to help rebuild domestic Jewish communities, Poland has not done so to near the same extent; and while Germany has focused on countering far-right ideology and membership, Poland has focused on emphasizing common connections between Poles and Jews. Despite antisemitism having such deep-seated roots in each country, the German and Polish approaches to confront the issue remain relatively new and unique in terms of addressing a social problem. Nonetheless, examining the practical implications of these efforts to this point offers opportunities to create more well-informed and improved strategies moving forward.

Practical Implications and Challenges

I have shown that the strategies implemented in the German and Polish cases have been more effective in achieving some goals than others. As of 2023, the strategies intended to counter antisemitism have tended to be more effective in improving general attitudes toward Jews and helping revive domestic Jewish communities than they have in reducing levels of antisemitic crimes. So, to answer one of the central research questions, one could say that indeed the strategies to counter antisemitism have been effective in reducing general antisemitic attitudes and less so in reducing antisemitic violence.

In both cases, general antisemitic attitudes declined by approximately half from the early 1990s to the early 2020s. These declines, especially in the Polish case, tended to follow the implementation of public diplomacy initiatives that were largely aimed toward achieving this goal. In Germany, these declines in general antisemitic attitudes were also marked by relatively consistent declines in far-right group membership—an area on which such campaigns tended to focus. In Poland, while general antisemitic attitudes tended to decline over time, there has been less progress in reducing the percentages of the population who believe certain religiously and economically antisemitic myths. Dispelling such myths has not tended to be a focus of the country's public diplomacy and is an area in clear need of improvement.

While Germany experienced some general declines in the number of antisemitic crimes from 2007 to 2017, there has been a sharp increase in the years since. An overwhelming number of such incidents have been perpetrated by those from a far-right ideology, and the country has responded by targeting most initiatives toward such groups. Nonetheless, the lack of progress in preventing the total number of antisemitic crimes shows an area in need of policy improvement. In Poland, it is more difficult to fully evaluate policy effectiveness regarding antisemitic crimes due to the scarcity of data on the subject. Such data is necessary to help determine which areas have been most successful and which need more improvement. Although the Polish Ministry of the Interior has published data on antisemitic crimes since 2016, the sample size is small when compared to Germany's. There is, however, little question among both countries' Jewish communities that antisemitism remains a major issue, with a 2018 EU Agency for Fundamental Rights (FRA) study showing that 85 percent of Jews in Germany and Poland responded that antisemitism remains either a "very big" or "fairly big" problem in their respective countries.

Nonetheless, both countries have experienced a revival of their domestic Jewish communities—Germany primarily in terms of population and Poland primarily in terms of the expression and popularity of Jewish culture. These revivals were not necessarily driven by the state, but each state has in part been responsible for facilitating the conditions necessary for a Jewish revival to take place. In Germany, a loosening of immigration laws for Jews has allowed the domestic Jewish population to grow rapidly. These measures were taken with an explicit intent to help revive domestic Jewish communities that had been decimated by the Holocaust. In Poland, the government has helped facilitate the revival of Jewish culture by helping finance Jewish cultural festivals and museums and by preserving and renovating Jewish historical sites. Such revivals serve the public diplomacy goals of each country by demonstrating progress and reconciliation with the Jewish community. These efforts have been complemented by more general outreach to Jewish communities not only domestically but abroad as well. German and Polish Jews are potentially credible messengers who can speak to this sort of domestic progress and help heal each country's reputation and image abroad. These sorts of outreach and strategic initiatives have been important components to each country's relationship with the Jewish community and public diplomacy—both domestically and abroad. However, such outreach and messaging must be complemented with domestic improvements to be deemed credible, and in this respect there remains significant room for progress.

Policy Recommendations

While both countries have demonstrated some progress on the issue of antisemitism as a result of their existing strategies, there are nonetheless areas for potential improvement. The data demonstrate that the policies targeting antisemitism in each country have been more effective in certain areas than others. On the whole, general antisemitic attitudes have declined in each country over time. To varying extents, each country has also experienced a revival of their respective Jewish communities. But there are still areas where either there is a lack of information or results have been less successful.

The first area for policy improvement is regarding data collection. One of the most severe problems in terms of fully grasping the problem of antisemitism in both countries is the reluctance that domestic Jewish communities have in reporting antisemitic harassment to police or other authorities. Survey data indicate that only about 20 percent of victims of antisemitic harassment reported the most serious incident they have experienced. This is alarming in that the crime data available is likely a vast undercount of the actual number of antisemitic incidents that have occurred. In order to improve the situation, the governments of both countries must build greater trust with their domestic Jewish communities. Only 22 percent of German Jews and 7 percent of Polish Jews believe their respective governments combat antisemitism effectively. To improve these numbers, government officials must first listen to their domestic Jewish communities to understand why this is the case. The EU FRA surveys on Jewish perceptions of antisemitism are particularly valuable in providing a snapshot of what domestic Jewish communities are experiencing and thinking with regard to antisemitism. Taking this a step further, each country's government must establish relationships with these communities to better understand the extent of antisemitic violence and harassment as well as what can be done. Few are more capable of understanding where the problem of antisemitism is arising and targeted than the victims themselves. For these reasons, domestic Jewish communities must be included when developing future solutions.

In addition to the problem of victim reporting, data collection must be improved in terms of its consistency and detail. In the Polish case, while general attitude data is collected with some consistency, more specific data measuring the particular manifestations of antisemitism tends to be collected infrequently. Moreover, hate crime data tends to be scarce and unreliable even though there has been some improvement since the establishment of a central police database in 2016. And while the data in the German case tends to be more prevalent and reliable, there are still areas in which it is lacking. For example, while general antisemitic crime data may be helpful in following trends in the aggregate, these data are not very helpful in terms of identifying the manifestations of antisemitism motivating the perpetrators nor the sources of their radicalization. Such information would be especially helpful in terms of better understanding what causes individuals to act and crafting solutions to mitigate the problem.

Improvements in these areas are especially important in a case such as Germany that has an increasingly diverse population. A one-size-fits-all approach to combating antisemitism may not be as effective as one that identifies the subtleties and different manifestations of the problem among different demographic groups. For example, the antisemitic myths and messaging among Muslim migrants in Germany tend to differ from the antisemitic myths and messaging among members of far-right political parties and groups. Strategies countering these beliefs would likely be more effective by tailoring their messaging to address these differences. Conducting regular (annual) survey research on antisemitic attitudes and their manifestations among different demographic groups as well as collecting more consistent and detailed hate crime data would greatly help in developing approaches to more directly target initiatives to counter antisemitism.

While there is certainly more information and study needed on the problem of antisemitism in each country, the existing data does present a few areas where Germany and Poland can most readily improve their strategies. In the German case, the data show general antisemitic attitudes declining over time, but xenophobic attitudes tend to be much more prevalent, especially in the former East Germany—a stronghold for far-right parties and groups. These rates of xenophobia remain a significant concern for Germany's domestic Jewish community, as some 90 percent are also immigrants. Combating xenophobia is likely to become more difficult and complex in the German case given recent influxes of Middle Eastern refugees and migrants and the popularity of conspiracy theories, such as the white replacement theory, which asserts that Jewish financing is responsible for such migration. Consequently, ensuring that efforts to combat antisemitism go hand-in-hand with efforts to combat xenophobia would likely provide a more effective and efficient means of reducing threats to Jewish communities.

Perhaps the most striking development in Germany in recent years has been the sharp increase in antisemitic attacks and crimes. Even as general antisemitic attitudes have declined over time, the level of antisemitic violence has reached new highs since 2018. Such a dynamic indicates that while improvements have been made in countering antisemitism within the general population, the same cannot be said of those willing to act on such beliefs. Programs such as Exit-Deutschland have shown some promise in removing members from far-right groups and preventing recidivism. However, whereas the Internet is the domain where the highest percentage of German Jews reported experiencing antisemitic harassment, there is no coordinated approach to countering antisemitism and radicalization in this space. Although the available data does not break down the sources of radicalization among perpetrators of antisemitic violence, there are indications that a greater number of violent actions are taken by individuals acting alone and who have been radicalized online, such as the 2019 Halle synagogue shooter.

While there are numerous challenges to countering antisemitic radicalization online, such as free speech, privacy, and jurisdictional issues, there are still steps that can be taken. One obvious recommendation is for social media and other technology companies to better moderate content on their platforms. However, such moderation is only likely to occur on certain platforms that have the resources and willingness to implement the necessary tools. Countering radicalization on darker and often unmoderated platforms is much more difficult but not impossible. A valuable resource in countering radicalization in these areas is former extremists, such as those served by the Exit-Deutschland program. Harnessing the expertise of those who best understand the platforms and techniques used to radicalize should be a priority in countering online antisemitism and extremism moving forward. Such individuals can also serve as effective messengers in countering the beliefs they once held. For these reasons, former antisemitic extremists can serve both directly and indirectly in developing improved approaches to countering the hatred they once perpetuated.

Given the vastness of the Internet, it is unrealistic to moderate all antisemitic content online, but another measure that can be taken to counter its spread is known as political or cultural jamming (sometimes referred to as guerrilla messaging). Jamming is a form of communication that is subversive, satirical, and often humorous with the goal of reinforcing an ideological message. This is a technique often used by extremist groups to spread their ideology and radicalize individuals online; however, the same technique can also be used to deconstruct antisemitic narratives. Social media is full of satirical cartoons, doctored photos, and humorous captions that promote ideological messages. These elements are also common to the idea of jamming. Penetrating the forums used by extremists to radicalize others online and injecting countermessaging through the use of jamming techniques provides a pathway to countering antisemitism online that is not impacted by free speech, privacy, or jurisdictional constraints. Jamming can be carried out by governmental or nongovernmental organizations swiftly and inexpensively. While the effectiveness of this technique has not yet been well studied, the tactic allows countermessaging to penetrate areas of the Internet that are otherwise difficult to reach. Therefore, jamming—a potentially promising strategy in the German case—is not limited by international borders and can be employed from anywhere in the world.

In the Polish case, like in the German, data have also shown improvement in terms of reducing general antisemitic attitudes. However, there have been notable increases in the percentages of Poles believing in certain antisemitic myths relating to blood libel, deicide, and economic antisemitism. These myths have been prevalent in Poland for centuries, yet Polish public diplomacy messaging does not tend to focus on countering these myths to any great extent. Poland's messaging often emphasizes common connections between Poles and Jews, and this messaging has been accompanied by increasing rates of sympathy among Poles toward Jews. A similar focus on countering antisemitic myths is perhaps the most pressing need in terms of addressing antisemitic attitudes within the country.

Poland has the infrastructure in place to develop and disseminate such messaging to counter antisemitic myths through organizations such as the Institute of National Remembrance, the Ministry of Foreign Affairs, and various other cultural institutions such as the POLIN museum. These organizations already work to correct mischaracterizations of Jewish history in the country and improve Polish-Jewish relations more generally; however, such organizations may not have the same credibility with those who hold religiously antisemitic beliefs. For this reason, grassroots efforts, ideally in partnership with thought leaders in the Catholic Church, could provide a more effective means of countering these sorts of beliefs. There have been instances, particularly involving the Catholic Church's Commission for Religious Relations with the Jews, where Catholic leaders have spoken out against antisemitism within the country, although such actions are often reactive. Pope John Paul II, perhaps the most widely beloved recent figure in Polish history, once described Jews as "our elder brothers" in faith (Vatican, 2000). Amplifying such sentiment within the church and across the country provides a pathway for better countering the oldest form of antisemitism within Poland.

While both Germany and Poland continue to grapple with the challenges and trauma of the Holocaust, each country has tended to take its own individual approach to countering antisemitism and reconciling with the past. Although both countries share a common history in many respects, they tend to have competing approaches to these issues rather than collaborative. Both countries share some similar themes in their approach, such as providing Judaism with certain legal protections, passing legislation to combat hate crimes, and engaging with NGOs to conduct public diplomacy; however, there has been little coordination between the two governments. Given the transnational nature of the

antisemitism problem, there are indeed opportunities for these governments to coordinate on certain issues and demonstrate a unified
approach to the problem. Although there are recurring tensions between
the two countries with regard to World War II and its aftermath, one
means of addressing such tensions and opening a dialogue would be the
establishment of an exchange program between the two countries for
the purposes of addressing the common threats of extremism, antisemitism, and xenophobia. Greater coordination may allow for opportunities to find common ground and develop potential solutions. Each
country already shares exchange agreements with other countries for
these purposes, notably the Forum for Dialogue Among Nations agreement with the American Jewish Committee, but there is not yet an
established program between Germany and Poland for these purposes.
Such an initiative could be complemented by joint dialogical forums
and similar events already hosted by each country. Involving influential policymakers, academics, and other public figures in such arrange-
ments would be an important step in relieving some of the tensions
between the countries and developing solutions to a problem that has
and continues to deeply affect both.

Avenues for Future Research

As the strategies examined throughout this book remain relatively new,
monitoring them in the future will provide greater insight into their
long-term effectiveness, especially as data becomes more plentiful in
this area. Both countries have organizations actively tracking survey
data on antisemitic attitudes, and Germany has consistently collected
crime data to evaluate. The lack of hate crime data in the Polish case
tends to be a limitation to this research; however, the recently established Interior Ministry database provides some promise. Also worthy
of further investigation is the dynamism and diversity of organizations
and partnerships that make up each country's public diplomacy, as these
may serve as a model for confronting social challenges in other cases.
And although the legal measures in each country have not experienced
many changes since the late 1990s and early 2000s, this too remains an
area worthy of future observation.

  In addition to examining these two cases, the analysis of other
postgenocide countries and regions will help add to the comparative
perspective on how to deal with similar problems most effectively. This
is true in comparing both the theoretical and practical implications of

legal and public diplomacy measures. Countries such as Turkey, Serbia, Cambodia, Guatemala, Rwanda, and others provide areas for comparison in terms of how these countries have attempted to resolve domestic tensions and improve international perceptions. Not all countries have approached these issues in the same way, so it would be useful to examine these differences to help find which measures have been most and least effective over time.

Pursuing these avenues of future research will help develop our understanding of the ways to reduce religious and ethnic hatred more generally. Antisemitism has been a historical problem in both the German and Polish cases and has marked each country's history and reputation as a result of the Holocaust. But antisemitism is a global problem, and there are many other forms of religious and ethnic hatred that exist around the world, so further examining their manifestations and the strategies to combat them may work to strengthen public policy and reduce violence and extremism going forward. In this book, I have offered a thorough examination of the efforts put forth by two countries marked by the most systematic genocide in human history. By examining these cases further and comparing them to relevant cases in other regions, we may discover improved ways to combat and prevent the forms of hatred and violence that continue to remain a problem throughout the world.

References

Abramsky, C., M. Jachimczyk, and A. Polonsky, eds. 1986. *The Jews in Poland.* Oxford: Blackwell.

Abramson, Henry. 2013. "Origins of Polish Jewry." Jewish History Lectures, December 5, 2013. http://jewishhistorylectures.org/2013/12/05/origins-of-polish-jewry-this-week-in-jewish-history/.

Adam Mickiewicz Institute. 2023. "Union of Jewish Religious Communities in Poland." http://www.diapozytyw.pl/en/site/organizacje/zwiazek.

Ahren, Raphael. 2014. "In First, Poland to Pay Reparations to Holocaust Survivors Abroad." *Times of Israel,* May 28.

Ain, Stewart. 2015. "New Pressure on Poland for Property Restitution." Jewish Telegraphic Agency, August 12. https://www.jta.org/2015/08/12/ny/new-pressure-on-poland-for-property-restitution.

Amadeu Antonio Stiftung. 2011. "Against Nazis in Mecklenburg-Vorpommern." https://www.amadeu-antonio-stiftung.de/gegen-nazis-in-mecklenburg-vorpommern-3457-7293/.

———. 2023a. "Empowerment, Youth Work, and Human-Rights Education." https://www.amadeu-antonio-stiftung.de/en/democratic-culture/.

———. 2023b. "Projektförderung." https://www.amadeu-antonio-stiftung.de/foerderung/.

———. 2023c. "Themes." https://www.amadeu-antonio-stiftung.de/en/themes/.

Ambrosewicz-Jacobs, Jolanta. 2013. "Antisemitism and Attitudes Toward the Holocaust: Empirical Studies from Poland." In *Proceedings of the Antisemitism in Europe Today: The Phenomena, the Conflicts Conference,* 1–9. Berlin: Jewish Museum of Berlin.

American Jewish Committee. 2018. "AJC Opposes Polish Effort to Criminalize Claims of Holocaust Responsibility." News release. January 27. https://www.prnewswire.com/news-releases/ajc-opposes-polish-effort-to-criminalize-claims-of-holocaust-responsibility-300589241.html.

Anti-Defamation League. 2005. "Attitudes Toward Jews in Twelve European Countries." May 2005. https://archive.jpr.org.uk/download?id=14255.

————. Various years. "Antisemitism Survey—Poland." https://global100.adl.org /#country/poland.

Arendt, Hannah. 1951. *The Origins of Totalitarianism.* New York: Schocken.

Aring, Paul Gerhard. 1998. "Werner von Oberwesel." In *Biographisch-Bibliographisches Kirchenlexikon,* vol. 13, edited by Traugott Bautz. Herzberg: Bautz.

Associated Press. 2014. "Epicenter of Holocaust Now Fastest-Growing Jewish Community." *Haaretz,* April 18. https://www.haaretz.com/jewish/2014-04 -08/ty-article/berlin-fastest-growing-jewish-community/0000017f-e1a9-d75c -a7ff-fdad19fd0000.

Auer, Claudia, and Alice Srugies. 2013. "Public Diplomacy in Germany." *Perspectives on Public Diplomacy* 5:1–56.

Bagger, Thomas. 2013. "Netzwerkpolitik." *Internationale Politik,* January 8.

Banas, J. 1979. *The Scapegoats, the Exodus and the Remnants of Polish Jewry.* London: Weidenfeld and Nicolson.

Baron, Salo Wittmayer. 1957. *Social and Religious History of the Jews,* vol. 4. New York: Columbia University Press, 1957.

Bartulin, Nevenko. 2013. *Honorary Aryans: National-Racial Identity and Protected Jews in the Independent State of Croatia.* London: Palgrave Macmillan.

Baumol, Avi. 2017. "Jonathan Ornstein Is Building a Jewish Community in Krakow!" *Times of Israel,* July 24.

Baur, Joe. 2022. "Looking for the Heart of Jewish Krakow." *Tablet,* July 19.

Bayzler, Michael. 2006. "Holocaust Denial Laws and Other Legislation Criminalizing Promotion of Nazism." Yad Vashem Institute for Holocaust Studies. https:// www.yadvashem.org/yv/en/holocaust/insights/pdf/bazyler.pdf.

BBC News. 2000. "Pope Prays for Holocaust Forgiveness." March 26. http://news .bbc.co.uk/onthisday/hi/dates/stories/march/26/newsid_4168000/4168803.stm.

Beit Polska. 2023. "Seeking Judaism, Step-By-Step." https://www.jewishrenewalinpoland .com/step-by-step/.

Belltower News. 2023. "Startseite." Home page. https://www.belltower.news/.

Ben-Rafael, Eliezer. 2015. "Germany's Russian Speaking Jews." In *Being Jewish in 21st Century Germany,* edited by Olaf Glöckner and Haim Fireberg. Berlin: de Gruyter.

Ben-Sasson, H., eds. 1976. *A History of the Jewish People.* Cambridge, MA: Harvard University Press.

Bergen, Doris L. 1996. *Twisted Cross: The German Christian Movement in the Third Reich.* Chapel Hill: University of North Carolina Press.

Bergmann, Werner. 1997. "Antisemitism and Xenophobia in Germany Since Unification." In Kurthen, Bergmann, and Erb 1997, 21–38.

Bergmann, Werner, and Rainer Erb. 1997. *Antisemitism in Germany: The Post-Nazi Epoch Since 1945.* New Brunswick, NJ: Transaction.

Bernhard, Michael, and Henryk Szlajfer. 2004. *From the Polish Underground.* University Park: University of Pennsylvania Press.

Bhatti, Jabeen. 2006. "Germany's Jews Mull Future as Immigration Drops." *Deutsche Welle,* November 27. http://www.dw.com/en/germanys-jews-mull-future-as -immigration-drops/a-2247891.

Bilewicz, Michał. 2012. "Antisemitism in Poland: Economic, Religious, and Historical Aspects." *Journal for the Study of Antisemitism* 4:2801–2820.

Black, E. 1987. "Lucien Wolf and the Making of Poland: Paris 1919." In *Polin,* vol. 2, edited by Antony Polonsky, 5–36. Liverpool: Liverpool University Press.

Borger, Julian, and Jeevan Vasagar. 2011. "A Jewish Renaissance in Poland." *Guardian* (UK edition), April 6.

Brendler, Konrad. 1994. "Die Holocaustrezeption der Enkelgeneration im Spannungsfeld von Abwehr und Traumatasierung." *Jahrbuch für Antisemitismusforschung* 3:303–340.

Bundestag. 2023. "Grundgesetz." https://www.bundestag.de/parlament/aufgaben/rechtsgrundlagen/grundgesetz.

Bylok, Katarzyna, and Konrad Pędziwiatr. 2010. "The Family of Radio Maryja and One of Its Activists." Academia. https://www.academia.edu/1498293/The_Family_of_Radio_Maryja_and_One_of_its_Activists.

Center for Research on Prejudice. 2023. "Polish Prejudice Survey." http://cbu.psychologia.pl/en/projekty/.

Central Statistical Office of Poland. 2020. "Religious Denominations in Poland 2015–2018." February 28, 2020. https://stat.gov.pl/en/topics/other-studies/religious-denominations/religious-denominations-in-poland-2015-2018,1,2.html.

Chambers, Madeline. 2017. "German AfD Rightist Triggers Fury with Holocaust Memorial Comments." Reuters, January 18.

———. 2022. "Anti-Jewish Medieval Sculpture Can Stay on Church, Top German Court Rules." Reuters, June 14.

Cichopek, Anna. 2003. "The Cracow Pogrom of August 1945: A Narrative Reconstruction." In *Contested Memories: Poles and Jews During the Holocaust and Its Aftermath*, edited by Joshua D. Zimmerman. New Brunswick, NJ: Rutgers University Press.

Cienski, Jan. 2020. "Poland's Presidential Campaign Ends on an Anti-Semitic Note." *Politico*, July 10.

CNN. 2023. "Catholic Church Honors Polish Family Persecuted for Sheltering Jews in Unprecedented Beatification." September 10.

Cohen, Jeremy. 2007. *Christ Killers: The Jews and the Passion from the Bible to the Big Screen.* Oxford: Oxford University Press.

Cohen, Roger. 2000. "Former Soviet Jews Find Uneasy Peace in Germany." *New York Times*, August 6.

Cohn-Sherbok, Dan. 2006. *The Paradox of Antisemitism.* New York: Continuum.

Cooper, Leo. 2000. *In the Shadow of the Polish Eagle.* New York: Palgrave.

Coordination Forum for Countering Antisemitism. 2014. "Poland Poll Reveals Stubborn Antisemitism Amid Jewish Revival Hopes." January 18. https://antisemitism.org.il/2014/01/18/article-84353-poland-poll-reveals-stubborn-antisemitism-amid-jewish-revival-hopes/.

Crossland, David. 2012. "We Can Resume Our Common History: New Paper Covers Revival of German Jewish Life." *Der Spiegel*, January 4.

Dawidowicz, L. 1983. *The Holocaust and the Historians.* Cambridge, MA: Harvard University Press.

Decker, Oliver, Johannes Kiess, Ayline Heller, and Elmar Brähler. 2022. *Autoritäte Dynamiken in Unsicheren Zeiten.* Leipzig: Psychosozial-Verlag.

Der Spiegel. 1996."Einwanderer: So Leise wie Möglich." May 26.

———. 2019. "Familienministerin Giffey will nun doch Exit-Programm fördern." October 17.

Deutsche Welle. 2005. "Neo-Nazis Spreading Message and Recruiting Through Music." December 12. http://www.dw-world.de/dw/article/0,2144,1827739,00.html.

———. 2008. "Supporting Judaism." September 25. http://www.dw.com/en/germany-boosts-financial-support-for-jewish-community/a-3669667.

———. 2010. "Jewish Revival." April 9. https://www.dw.com/en/mainz-synagogue-highlights-revival-of-jewish-life-in-germany/a-5974508.

————. 2018. "Synagogues in Germany." November 8. http://www.dw.com/en /synagogues-in-germany/g-18208619.

————. 2019. "Germany: First Postwar Kosher Restaurant Opens in Leipzig." March 27. https://www.dw.com/en/germany-first-postwar-kosher-restaurant -opens-in-leipzig/a-48083120.

Die Welt. 2012. "Türkische Migranten Hoffen auf Muslimische Mehrheit." August 17.

Dimont, Max I. 2004. *Jews, God, and History.* London: Penguin.

Downs, Robert. 2004. *Books That Changed the World.* New York: Signet.

Dubnow, Sidney. 2001. *History of the Jews in Russia and Poland.* Skokie: Varda.

Eddy, Melissa, Rick Gladstone, and Tiffany Tsu. 2019. "Assailant Live-Streamed Attack on German Synagogue." *New York Times,* October 9.

Ehrenreich, Eric. 2007. *The Nazi Ancestral Proof: Genealogy, Racial Science, and the Final Solution.* Bloomington: Indiana University Press.

Eidelberg, Shlomo, eds. 1977. *The Jews and the Crusaders.* Madison: University of Wisconsin Press.

Ellis, Marc H. 2004. "Hitler and the Holocaust, Christian Antisemitism." Slide 14. Baylor University Center for American and Jewish Studies.

EU Agency for Fundamental Rights. 2015. "Antisemitism: Overview of Data Available in the European Union." http://fra.europa.eu/sites/default/files/fra_uploads /fra-2015-antisemitism-update_en.pdf.

————. 2018. "Experiences and Perceptions of Antisemitism." https://archive.jpr .org.uk/download?id=3650.

Eurobarometer. 2000. "Percentage in Favor of Potential Candidate Countries." https://europa.eu/eurobarometer/surveys/browse/all/series/4961.

European Parliamentary Research Service. 2020. "The European Union and Holocaust Remembrance." https://www.europarl.europa.eu/RegData/etudes/BRIE /2018/614662/EPRS_BRI(2018)614662_EN.pdf.

Exit-Deutschland. 2023a. "EXIT-Germany: We Provide Ways Out of Extremism," http://www.exit-deutschland.de/english/.

————. 2023b. "Über Uns." https://www.exit-deutschland.de/exit/?c=ueber-unsx.

Federal Association of Departments for Research and Information on Antisemitism. 2023."About RIAS Federal Foundation." https://report-antisemitism.de/en /bundesverband-rias/.

Federal Ministry of the Interior. 2018. "Strengthening the Jewish Community in Germany." https://www.bmi.bund.de/SharedDocs/kurzmeldungen/EN/2018/07 /zentralrat-der-juden.html.

————. 2023a. "Federal Government Commissioner for Jewish Life in Germany and the Fight Against Antisemitism." https://www.bmi.bund.de/EN/ministry /commissioners/antisemitism/antisemitism-node.html.

————. 2023b. "National Strategy Against Antisemitism and for Jewish Life." https://www.bmi.bund.de/SharedDocs/downloads/EN/publikationen/2023 /BMI23001.pdf?__blob=publicationFile&v=6.

Federal Office for Protection of the Constitution. Various years. "Annual Report from the Federal Office for Protection of the Constitution (*Verfassungsschutzbericht*)." https://www.verfassungsschutz.de/DE/verfassungsschutz/der -bericht/der-bericht_node.html.

Ferber, Alona. 2014. "Historical Milestone: Theology School Symbol of Revival of Jewish Life." *Der Spiegel,* February 20.

Forum for Dialogue Among Nations. 2023. "Polish-Jewish Exchange Program." http://dialog.org.pl/en/polishjewish-exchange-program/.

Foundation for the Preservation of Jewish Heritage in Poland. 2023. "About Us." http://fodz.pl/?d=3&l=en.

Foundation of the Jewish Museum Berlin. 2010. *Highlights from the Jewish Museum Berlin.* Berlin: Nicolai-Verlag.

Friedman, Jonathan. 2012. *Jewish Communities of Europe on the Eve of World War II.* New York: Routledge.

Fulbrook, Mary. 1999. *German National Identity After the Holocaust.* Cambridge, UK: Polity.

Gensicke, Klaus. 2007. *Der Mufti von Jerusalem und die Nationalsozialisten.* Darmstadt: Wissenschaftliche Buchgesellschaft.

German Federal Foreign Office. 1999. *Auswärtige Kulturpolitik—Konzeption 2000.* Berlin: Auswärtiges Amt [Federal Foreign Office].

German Ministry of the Interior. Various years. "Annual Report on Politically Motivated Crime (*Politische Motivierte Kriminalität*)." https://www.bmi.bund.de/DE/themen/sicherheit/kriminalitaetsbekaempfung-und-gefahrenabwehr/politisch-motivierte-kriminalitaet/politisch-motivierte-kriminalitaet-node.html.

German Ministry of Justice. 2023. "Strafgesetzbuch." https://www.gesetze-im-internet.de/englisch_stgb/.

Gesemann, Frank. 2006. "Die Integration junger Muslime in Deutschland." In *Interkultureller Dialog—Islam und Gesellschaft,* no. 5. Berlin: Friedrich Ebert Foundation.

Golb, Norman. 1998. *The Jews in Medieval Normandy: A Social and Intellectual History.* Cambridge: Cambridge University Press.

Grisar, P. J. 2020. "Poland's Jewish Museum Director Is Stepping Aside—Why Now?" *Forward,* February 14.

Grollmus, Denise. 2012. "Poland's Real Jewish Revival." *Tablet,* November 26.

Gross, Jan. 1979. *Polish Society Under Occupation: The Generalgouvernment 1939–1945.* Princeton, NJ: Princeton University Press.

———. 2007. *Fear: Antisemitism in Poland After Auschwitz.* New York: Random House.

Guardian. 2018. "Polish Law Denies Reality of Holocaust." *Guardian* (US edition), February 5.

Gutman, Y., E. Mendelsohn, and Ch. Shmeruk, eds. 1989. *The Jews of Poland Between Two World Wars.* Hanover, NH: University Press of New England.

Haaretz. 2003. "Germany's Jews Sign Historic Pact; France Torn by Talk of Anti-Semitism." January 28.

Herf, Jeffrey. 2013. *Antisemitism and Anti-Zionism in Historical Perspective: Convergence and Divergence.* London: Routledge.

Hitler, Adolf. 1998. *Mein Kampf.* Translated by Ralph Mannheim. Boston: Houghton Mifflin. This translation first published 1943.

Hundert, Gershon. 1986. "The Implications of Jewish Economic Activities for Christian-Jewish Relations in the Polish Commonwealth." In Abramsky, Jachimczyk, and Polonsky, 55–63. Oxford: Blackwell.

———. 2004. *Jews in Poland-Lithuania in the Eighteenth Century: A Genealogy of Modernity.* Berkeley: University of California Press.

Institute for Jewish Policy Research. 2023. "Germany: How Many Jews Live in Germany?" https://www.jpr.org.uk/countries/how-many-jews-in-germany.

Institute of National Remembrance. 2023a. "Act on the Institute of National Remembrance." https://ipn.gov.pl/en.

———. 2023b. "Offices." https://ipn.gov.pl/en/about-the-institute/offices.

———. 2023c. "Home Page," https://ipn.gov.pl/en.

International Holocaust Remembrance Alliance. 2023. "What Is Antisemitism?" https://www.holocaustremembrance.com.

Jarosz, Andy. 2013. "New Life in Krakow's Jewish Quarter." *BBC*, February 17.

Jerusalem Declaration on Antisemitism. 2023. "The Jerusalem Declaration on Antisemitism." https://jerusalemdeclaration.org/.

Jeske-Choiński, Teodor. 1913. *Poznaj Piastow.* Warsaw: Panstowowy Instytut Wydawniczy.

Jewish Community Center of Krakow. 2022. "Our Story." http://www.jcckrakow.org /subpages/1.

Jewish Community of Berlin. 2012. "Jüdische Kulturtage 2012." http://www.jg-berlin.org/fileadmin/redaktion/downloads/JKT_2012_Programmheft.pdf.

―――. 2023a. "Days of Jewish Culture." http://www.jg-berlin.org/en/institutions /culture/juedische-kulturtage.html.

―――. 2023b. "Integration." http://www.jg-berlin.org/en/institutions/integration.html.

Jewish Heritage Europe. 2016. "Poland: More Funding for Przysucha Synagogue Restoration."

Jewish Museum Berlin. 2023a. "History of Our Museum."

―――. 2023b. "The W. Michael Blumenthal Academy of the Jewish Museum Berlin."

Jewish Telegraphic Agency. 2016. "Polish Jewry Museum Wins European Museum of the Year Award." http://www.jta.org/2016/04/10/news-opinion/world/polish -jewry-museum-wins-european-museum-of-the-year-award.

Jewish Virtual Library. 2023. "Virtual Jewish History Tour: Poland." http:// www.jewishvirtuallibrary.org/jsource/vjw/Poland.html.

Jikeli, Günther. 2015. "Antisemitic Attitudes Among Muslims in Europe: A Survey Review." Institute for the Study of Global Antisemitism and Policy, May 2015. https://isgap.org/wp-content/uploads/2015/05/Jikeli_Antisemitic_Attitudes _among_Muslims_in_Europe1.pdf.

Johnson, Paul. 1988. *A History of the Jews.* New York: Harper Perennial.

Kamen, Henry. 1998. *The Spanish Inquisition: A Historical Revision.* New Haven, CT: Yale University Press.

Karten, Britt Inga. 2008. "Staatliche Imagearbeit: Die Public Diplomacy des Auswärtigen Amtes." In *Die amerikanische Regierung gegen die Weltöffentlichkeit? Theoretische und empirische Analysen der Public Diplomacy zum Irakkrieg,* edited by Thomas Jäger and Henrike Viehrig, 163–190. Wiesbaden: VS Verlag für Sozialwissenschaften.

Katz, Jacob. 1969."A State Within a State: The History of an Antisemitic Slogan." *Proceedings of the Israel Academy of Sciences and Humanities,* vol. 4, no. 3. Jerusalem: Israel Academy of Sciences and Humanities.

Katzenstein, Peter. 1997. "United Germany in an Integrating Europe." In *Tamed Power: Germany in Europe,* edited by Peter Katzenstein. Ithaca: Cornell University Press.

Kirschbaum, Erik, and Bethan John. 2014. "At a Landmark Berlin Rally, Merkel Vows to Fight Antisemitism." Reuters, September 14.

Klein, David. 2023. "In First, Polish Priest Sentenced on Charges of Spreading Antisemitic Hate Speech," *Times of Israel,* February 13.

Klusmeyer, Douglas, and Demetrios Papademetriou. 2013. *Immigration Policy in the Federal Republic of Germany.* New York: Berghahn.

Korey, William. 1995. *Russian Antisemitism, Pamyat, and the Demonology of Zionism.* London: Routledge.

Kozielski, Maciej. 2023. "Wieczorami Eska, Trójka i Radio Maryja ze wzrostem słuchalności. Badanie Radio." Press. May 22, 2023. https://www.press.pl/tresc

/76644,radio-track_-wieczorami-eska_-trojka-i-radio-maryja-ze-wzrostem -sluchalnosci.

Kreutzmüller, Christoph. 2012. *Final Sale—The Destruction of Jewish Owned Businesses in Nazi Berlin 1930–1945.* Berlin: Metropol-Verlag.

Kucia, M. 2010. *Antysemityzm w Polsce a.d. 2010.* Warsaw: OBOP.

Kulczycki, John. 2005. "Eastern Europe in Western Civilization Textbooks: The Example of Poland." *History Teacher* 38 (2): 163–167.

Kunicki, Mikołaj. 2012. *Between the Brown and Red: Nationalism, Catholicism, and Communism in 20th Century Poland.* Athens: Ohio University Press.

Kurthen, Hermann, Werner Bergmann, and Rainer Erb, eds. 1997. *Antisemitism and Xenophobia in Germany After Unification.* New York: Oxford University Press.

Lang, Berel. 2009. *Philosophical Witness: The Holocaust as Presence.* Waltham, MA: Brandeis University Press.

Laqueur, Walter. 2006. *The Changing Face of Antisemitism: From Ancient Times to the Present Day.* Oxford: Oxford University Press.

Lazare, Bernard. 1903. *Antisemitism: Its History and Causes.* New York: International Library.

Lazaroff, Tovah. 2020. "Duda's Fateful Polish Victory a Mixed Bag for Jews, Israel." *Jerusalem Post,* July 14.

Leonard, Mark, Catherine Stead, and Conrad Smewing. 2002. *Public Diplomacy.* London: Public Diplomacy Centre.

Levin, Nora. 1968. *The Holocaust: The Destruction of European Jewry 1933–1945.* New York: T. Y. Crowell.

Levy, Richard. 2005. *Antisemitism: A Historical Encyclopedia or Prejudice and Persecution.* Santa Barbara, CA: ABC-CLIO.

Lewis, Bernard. 1999. *Semites and Anti-Semites: An Inquiry into Conflict and Prejudice.* New York: W. W. Norton.

Liang, Christina Schori. 2013. *Europe for the Europeans: The Foreign and Security Policy of the Populist Radical Right.* Farnham, UK: Ashgate.

Lichten, J. 1986. "Notes on the Assimilation and Acculturation of Jews in Poland 1863–1943." In Abramsky, Jachimczyk, and Polonsky, 106–129. Oxford: Blackwell.

Lieu, Judith, John North, and Tessa Rajak. 2013. *The Jews Among Pagans and Christians in the Roman Empire.* London: Routledge.

Linse, Ulrich. 2014. "Völkisch-jugendbewegte Siedlungen im 20. Und 21. Jahrhundert." In *Jugendbewegung, Antisemitismus und Rechtsradikale Politik,* edited by Gideon Botsch and Josen Haverkamp, 29–73. Berlin: De Gruyter.

Lukas, Richard. 1986. *The Forgotten Holocaust, the Poles Under German Occupation 1939–1944.* Lexington: University Press of Kentucky.

Luther, Martin. 1971. *On the Jews and Their Lies.* Translated by Martin H. Bertram. Philadelphia: Fortress Press.

Mahler, R. 1942. *Antisemitism in Poland: Essays on Antisemitism.* New York: Conference on Jewish Relations.

Marsden, Victor. 2014. *Protocols of the Learned Elders of Zion.* Bensonville, IL: Lushena Books.

Martin, Gus. 2015. *Understanding Terrorism: Challenges, Perspectives, and Issues.* Thousand Oaks, CA: SAGE Publications.

Mayer, Ayla. 2015. "Ein Euro pro Hassposting: Rassisten sammeln unfreiwillig für Flüchtlinge." *Der Spiegel,* October 23.

Merriam-Webster Dictionary. 2023. "Antisemitism."

Michael, Robert. 2006. *Holy Hatred: Christianity, Antisemitism, and the Holocaust.* New York: Palgrave Macmillan.

Murphy, Cullen. 2012. *God's Jury: The Inquisition and the Making of the Modern World*. Boston: Houghton Mifflin Harcourt.

Mut gegen rechte Gewalt. 2023. "Über Uns." http://www.mut-gegen-rechte-gewalt.de/.

National Catholic Reporter. 2018. "Jewish Leader: Polish Church Should Speak Out as Anti-Semitism Rises." March 7. https://www.ncronline.org/news/jewish-leader-polish-church-should-speak-out-anti-semitism-rises.

National Electoral Commission of Poland. 2023. "Election Results." http://pkw.gov.pl.

Nicholson, Esme. 2018. "Meet the Jews of the German Far-Right." National Public Radio, October 21.

Niedermayer, Oskar. 2016. "Parteimitglieder in Deutschland: Version 2016." Freie Universität Berlin. https://refubium.fu-berlin.de/handle/fub188/18704.

Noor, M., J. R. Brown, and G. Prentice. 2008. "Precursors and Mediators of Intergroup Reconciliation in Northern Ireland: A New Model." *British Journal of Social Psychology* 47:481–495.

Nye, Joseph. 2008. "Public Diplomacy and Soft Power." *Annals of the American Academy of Political and Social Science* 616 (1): 94–109.

Ociepka, Beata. 2012. "Polish Public Diplomacy." *E-International Relations*, October 8. https://www.e-ir.info/2012/10/08/polish-public-diplomacy/.

Ociepka, Beata, and Marta Ryniejska. 2005. "Public Diplomacy and EU Enlargement: The Case of Poland." Netherlands Institute of International Relations. http://www.clingendael.org/sites/default/files/pdfs/20050800_cli_paper_dip_issue99.pdf.

Olick, Jeffrey, and Andrew Perrin. 2010. *Guilt and Defense*. Cambridge, MA: Harvard University Press.

Orlicki, J. 1983. *Szkice z djiejow stosunkow polsko-zydowskich*. Szczecin: Krajowa Agencja Wydawnicza.

OSCE. 2023a. "Hate Crime Reporting: Poland." Organization for Security and Co-operation in Europe. https://hatecrime.osce.org/poland.

———. 2023b. "National Frameworks to Address Hate Crime in Poland." Organization for Security and Co-operation in Europe. https://hatecrime.osce.org/national-frameworks-poland#dataCollection.

Ostermann, Dietmar. 2013. "Aussteiger Initiative 'Exit' Kann Weitermachen." *Badische Zeitung*, March 22. http://www.badische-zeitung.de/deutschland-1/aussteiger-initiative-exit-kann-weitermachen—70249792.html.

Pearson, Karl. 1924. *The Life, Letters, and Labours of Francis Galton*. Cambridge: Cambridge University Press, 1924.

Peck, Jeffrey. 2006. *Being Jewish in the New Germany*. New Brunswick, NJ: Rutgers University Press.

Penslar, Derek Jonathan. 2001. *Shylock's Children: Economics and Jewish Identity in Modern Europe*. Berkeley: University of California Press.

Petrovsky-Shtern, Yohanan. 2009. *Jews in the Russian Army 1827–1917—Drafted into Modernity*. Cambridge: Cambridge University Press.

Pew Research Center. 2006. "Global Attitudes and Trends." http://www.pewglobal.org/category/datasets/2006/?download=12029.

Pietikäinen, Petteri. 2000. "The 'Volk' and Its Unconscious: Jung, Hauer and the 'German Revolution.'" *Journal of Contemporary History* 35 (4): 523–539.

Piotrowski, Tadeusz. 1997. *Poland's Holocaust*. Jefferson, NC: McFarland and Company.

Pipes, Daniel. 1997. *Conspiracy: How the Paranoid Style Flourishes and Where It Comes From*. New York: Simon & Schuster.

Plucinska, Joanna. 2020. "Poland Names New Head of Jewish Museum as Tensions Rise." *Reuters*, February 27.

Poliakov, Leon. 1974. *The History of Antisemitism*. New York: Vanguard Press.

POLIN Museum. 2022. "Anniversary of the Opening of the Core Exhibition: More than Two Million Visitors and Counting." October 27. https://www.polin.pl/en/aktualnosci/2022/10/27/anniversary-of-the-core-exhibition.

———. 2023. "About the Museum." https://www.polin.pl/en/about-the-museum.

Polish Ministry of Culture. 2009. "The Construction of the Museum of the History of Polish Jews." http://mkidn.gov.pl/pages/posts/rozpoczeto_budowe_muzeum_historii_zydow_polskich-196.php.

———. 2023. "Cultural Seasons and Major Events." http://www.mkidn.gov.pl/pages/the-ministry-of-culture-and-national-heritage/cultural-seasons-and-major-events.php.

Polish Ministry of Foreign Affairs. 2012. "Public Diplomacy 2012." http://www.culturaldiplomacy.org/academy/pdf/research/books/public_diplomacy/Public_Diplomacy_-_Ministry_Of_Foreign_Affairs_Of_The_Republic_Of_Poland.pdf.

———. 2023a. "Polish Diaspora and Poles Abroad Day." https://www.gov.pl/web/diplomacy/polish-diaspora-and-poles-abroad-day.

———. 2023b. "Public Diplomacy." https://www.gov.pl/web/diplomacy/public-diplomacy.

Polish Ministry of the Interior. 2023. "The Repatriation Act of 9 November 2000." https://archiwum.mswia.gov.pl/en/document/the-repatriation-act-o/28,The-Repatriation-Act-of-9-November-2000.html.

Polish Penal Code. 1997. "The Penal Code." https://www.imolin.org/doc/amlid/Poland_Penal_Code1.pdf.

Polish Sejm. 2023. "The Constitution of the Republic of Poland of April 2, 1997." https://www.sejm.gov.pl/prawo/konst/angielski/kon1.htm.

Prekerowa, T. 1992. *Zarys dziejow Zydow w Polsce w latach 1939–1945*. Warsaw: Wydawnictwo Uniwersytetu Warszawskiego.

Public Opinion Research Center. 2021. "Polish Public Opinion." November. https://www.cbos.pl/PL/publikacje/public_opinion/2021/11_2021.pdf.

———. Various years. "Annual Public Opinion Survey." https://www.cbos.pl/EN/publications/public_opinion.php.

Puhl, Jan. 2006. "Papal Reprimand for Catholic Radio." *Der Spiegel*, May 2.

Rees, Laurence. 2012. *The Dark Charisma of Adolf Hitler*. London: Ebury Press.

Remennick, L. 2005. "'Idealists Headed to Israel, Pragmatics Chose Europe': Identity Dilemmas and Social Incorporation Among Former Soviet Jews Who Immigrated to Germany." *Immigrants and Minorities* 23 (1): 30–58.

Rensmann, Lars. 2004. "Collective Guilt, National Identity, and Political Processes in Contemporary Germany." In *Collective Guilt: International Perspectives,* edited by Nyla Branscombe and Bertjan Doosje, 169–190. Cambridge: Cambridge University Press.

Rietschel, Matthias. 2006. "Nazi Racial Purity Exhibit Opens in Germany." MSNBC, October 9.

Rigg, Bryan Mark. 2002. *Hitler's Jewish Soldiers: The Untold Story of Nazi Racial Laws and Men of Jewish Descent in the German Military*. Lawrence: Kansas University Press.

Riley-Smith, Jonathan. 1991. *The First Crusade and the Idea of Crusading*. Philadelphia: University of Pennsylvania Press.

Ringelblum, E. 1985. *Writings from the Warsaw Ghetto*, vol. 1. Tel Aviv: Peretz.

Rittberger, Volker, and Wolfgang Wagner. 2001. "German Foreign Policy Since Unification—Theories Meet Reality." In *German Foreign Policy Since Unification: Theories and Case Studies,* edited by Volker Rittberger, 299–326. Manchester, UK: Manchester University Press.

Rudnicki, S. 1987. "From 'Numerus Clausus' to 'Numerus Nullus.'" In *Polin,* vol. 2, edited by Antony Polonsky, 246–268. Liverpool: Liverpool University Press.

Rzeczpospolita. 2023. "Priest Convicted for Preaching. The First Such Verdict." https://www.rp.pl/prawo-karne/art37907491-ksiadz-skazany-za-kazanie-pierwszy-taki-wyrok.

Sachar, Howard Morley. 2005. *A History of the Jews in the Modern World.* New York: Random House.

Salzborn, Samuel. 2018. "Antisemitism in the 'Alternative for Germany' Party." *German Politics and Society,* 36 (3): 74–93.

Samuel, Sigal. 2018. "Why a Small Jewish Group Is Supporting a German Party with Antisemitic Ties." *Atlantic,* October 7.

Schaechter, Rukhl. 2007. "Krakow Jewish Fest Features Notable Absence: Jews." *Forward,* July 13.

Schreckenburg, Heinz. 1996. *The Jews in Christian Art.* New York: Continuum.

Schultz, Joseph. 1982. *Judaism and the Gentile Faiths: Comparative Studies in Religion.* Teaneck, NJ: Fairleigh Dickinson University Press.

Schwartz, Yardena. 2019. "40 Miles from Auschwitz, Poland's Jewish Community is Beginning to Thrive." *Time,* February 27.

Schweitzer, Frederick, and Marvin Perry. 2002. *Antisemitism: Myth and Hate from Antiquity to the Present.* London: Palgrave Macmillan.

Segel, Binjamin and Richard Levy. 1996. *A Lie and Libel: The History of the Protocols of the Elders of Zion.* Lincoln: University of Nebraska Press.

Smolar, A. 1987. "Jews as a Polish Problem." *Daedalus* 116 (2): 31–73.

Statistics Poland. 2019. *Concise Statistical Yearbook of Poland.* Warsaw: Republic of Poland.

Stirk, Peter. 2002. "Hugo Preuss, German Political Thought and the Weimar Constitution." *History of Political Thought* 23 (3): 497–516.

Stola, Dariusz. 2012. "Poland's Institute of National Remembrance: An Institute of Memory?" In *The Convolutions of Historical Politics,* edited by A. Miller and M. Lipman, 45–58. Budapest: Central European University Press.

Strack, Christoph. 2018. "Berlin: Where Jews Want to Live." Deutsche Welle, November 9. https://www.dw.com/en/berlin-where-jews-want-to-live/a-46229120.

Sulek, Antoni. 2012. "Ordinary Poles Look at the Jews." *East European Politics and Society* 26 (2): 425–444.

Susskind, Toni. 2016. "Q+A with Jonathan Ornstein." *J-Wire,* April 7. https://www.jwire.com.au/qa-jonathan-ornstein/.

Swart, Bert. 2001. "Denying Shoah." In *Personal Autonomy, the Private Sphere and Criminal Law: A Comparative Study,* edited by Peter Alldridge and Chrisje Brants, 161–180. New York: Bloomsbury.

Syal, Rajeev. 2015. "Polish Defence Minister Condemned over Jewish Conspiracy Theory." *Guardian* (US edition), November 10.

Tegel, Susan. 2011. *The Jew Süss: His Life and Afterlife in Legend, Literature and Film.* London: Continuum.

Times of Israel. 2013. "82 Attacks in Four Years on German Synagogues." October 21.

———. 2018a. "Full Text of Poland's Controversial Holocaust Legislation." February 1.

————. 2018b. "Yad Vashem: Poland's Holocaust Law Risks 'Serious Distortion' of Complicity." January 27.

Todeschini, Giacomo. 2004. "Franciscan Economics and Jews." In *Friars and Jews in the Middle Ages and Renaissance*, vol. 2, edited by Susan E. Myers and Steven J. McMichael, 99–118. Leiden, Netherlands: Brill.

Tomaszewski, I., and T. Werbowski. 1994. *Zegota, The Rescue of Jews in Wartime Poland*. Montreal: Price-Patterson.

Tomicki, J. 1982. *Polska odrodzona*. Warsaw: Wiedza Powszechna.

Tzur, Nissan. 2012. "Recent Converts Offer a Glimpse of Judaism's Appeal in Poland." *Times of Israel*, November 4.

————. 2013. "25th Jewish Culture Festival Brings Sabra Style to Krakow." *Jerusalem Post*, June 30.

UNESCO. 2007. "World Heritage Committee Approves Auschwitz Name Change."

US Department of State. 2022. "2021 Report on International Religions Freedom: Poland." https://www.state.gov/reports/2021-report-on-international-religious-freedom/poland/.

————. 2023. "International Religious Freedom Reports." https://www.state.gov/report/custom/7e1482be57/.

US Holocaust Memorial Museum. 2023a. "The German Churches and the Nazi State." http://www.ushmm.org/wlc/en/article.php?ModuleId=10005206.

————. 2023b. "Germany: Jewish Population in 1933." https://encyclopedia.ushmm.org/content/en/article/germany-jewish-population-in-1933.

————. 2023c. "Jewish Population of Europe in 1945." http://www.ushmm.org/wlc/en/article.php?ModuleId=10005687.

van Ham, Peter. 2008. "Place Branding: The State of the Art." *Annals of the American Academy of Political and Social Science* 616:126–149.

Vatican. 2000. "The Roots of Anti-Judaism in the Christian Environment." https://www.vatican.va/jubilee_2000/magazine/documents/ju_mag_01111997_p-42x_en.html.

Virtual Jewish Library. 2023. "Virtual Jewish World: Leipzig, Germany." http://www.jewishvirtuallibrary.org/jsource/judaica/ejud_0002_0012_0_12095.html.

Wagner, Richard. 1869. *Das Judenthum in der Musik*. Leipzig: Weber.

Wahlrecht.de website. 2023. "Election Results." http://www.wahlrecht.de/.

Webb, James. 1976. *The Occult Establishment*. La Salle, IL: Open Court.

Weil, Frederick. 1997. "Ethnic Intolerance, Extremism, and Democratic Attitudes in Germany Since Unification." In Kurthen, Bergmann, and Erb 1997, 110–142.

Wetzel, Juliane. 1997. "Antisemitism Among Right-Wing Extremist Groups, Organizations, and Parties in Postunification Germany." In Kurthen, Bergmann, and Erb 1997, 143–173.

Whine, Michael. 2008. "Expanding Holocaust Denial and Legislation Against It." *Jewish Political Studies Review* 20 (1): 57–77.

Williams, Rob. 2013. "'Nazi Shazam': German Authorities Plan to Use App to Identify Banned Neo-Nazi Music at Rallies." *Independent*, December 3.

Wilson, William. 1973. "Herder Folklore and Romantic Nationalism." *Journal of Popular Culture* 6 (4): 819–835.

Wistrich, Robert. 2012. *Holocaust Denial: The Politics of Perfidy*. Berlin: de Gruyter.

Wolffsohn, Michael. 1993. *Eternal Guilt?: Forty Years of German-Jewish-Israeli Relations*. New York: Columbia University Press.

World Jewish Restitution Organization. 2023. "Restitution by Country: Poland." https://wjro.org.il/our-work/restitution-by-country/poland/.

Yivo Institute for Jewish Research. 2023a. "Poland Since 1939." http://www
.yivoencyclopedia.org/article.aspx/poland/poland_since_1939.

———. 2023b. "Population and Migration: Population Since World War I." http://
www.yivoencyclopedia.org/article.aspx/Population_and_Migration.

Zentrum Demokratische Kultur. 2023. "Startseite." http://zentrum-demokratische
-kultur.de/start/.

Zubrzycki, Genevieve. 2006. *The Crosses of Auschwitz: Nationalism and Religion
in Post-Communist Poland.* Chicago: University of Chicago Press.

———. 2012. "Religion, Religious Tradition, and Nationalism: Jewish Revival in
Poland and 'Religious Heritage' in Quebec." *Journal for the Scientific Study of
Religion* 51 (3): 442–455.

Zychowicz, Peter. 2005. "Interview with the Minister of Foreign Affairs of the
Republic of Poland, Prof. Adam Daniel Rotfeld." *Rzeczpospolita*, January 25.
https://web.archive.org/web/20080627030817/http://www.msz.gov.pl/gallery
/serwis/rot_rzecz_1251.html.

Index

About the Book

IN BOTH GERMANY AND POLAND—PRIMARY LOCATIONS OF THE HOLO-
caust—the legacy of antisemitism remains a major obstacle to reconciliation with the past. Thomas Just asks: How does antisemitism typically
manifest in these countries? What counterstrategies are being employed?
And with what effect? Addressing these questions, Just contributes to a
deeper understanding of the disturbing influence of antisemitic hatred
worldwide and identifies best practices to combat it.

Thomas Just is assistant teaching professor in the school of Politics
and Global Studies at Arizona State University.